PRESIDENT REED

OF

PENNSYLVANIA.

A REPLY TO

MR. GEORGE BANCROFT AND OTHERS.

"Who, that knows anything of literary history or of society, cannot recall a number of cases, where slander, however base and baseless, has been believed to be true, for no other reason than because it has never been contradicted? Nay, a calumny may have been buried in obscurity for centuries and millenaries, and at length some literary truffle dog will hunt it out; and, if it do but concern some great man, the vulgar will pelt it at his head."—HARE'S VINDICATION OF NIEBUHR.

FEBRUARY, A. D. 1867.

THIRD EDITION.

PHILADELPHIA:
HOWARD CHALLEN, 1308 CHESTNUT STREET.
JOHN CAMPBELL, 740 SANSOM STREET.

Entered, according to the Act of Congress, in the year 1867,
By WILLIAM B. REED,
in the Clerk's office of the District Court of the United States in and for the
Eastern District of Pennsylvania.

W. P. KILDARE, PRINTER.

INTRODUCTION.

It will be apparent to every reader of the following pages that the historical materials they illustrate have not been recently collected. Most of them have been in my possession for many years, but for reasons which I have frankly stated, were not used. Indeed, but for Mr. Bancroft's late volume, which literally is the straw which broke the back of my endurance, they would not be used now. His book however, renders it necessary that I should break my silence. To those who think it would have been better had I not opened the whole subject of the attacks on Mr. Reed, but confined myself to Mr. Bancroft's share of them, I suggest that, dealing as I am with at least one unscrupulous adversary, it would be hazardous to leave for his use the testimony, such as it is, of past times, and thus subject myself to the necessity of a rejoinder. Though Mr. Bancroft, with the exception of a single and unaccredited quotation, is silent as to the Pamphlets of the last century, he knows all about them, and had I answered the Donop fiction alone, he would have brought them forward as his fresh reserve. I had no alternative but to discuss the whole subject, and I have endeavoured to exhaust it.

Chestnut Hill, January, 1867.   W. B. Reed.

MORE than eighty years after my ancestor was laid in his honoured grave, I am called on to vindicate his name. Instead of partisan misrepresentation (to use a mild word,) being allowed to die with the passions of a period of revolutionary excitement, it has been industriously kept alive, until at last, in the second and almost the third generation, the necessity of correcting and repelling it has arisen. There is, in this country, a class of men, happily not numerous, who take pleasure in disparaging the accredited patriots of the first revolution. They do so either from hereditary or personal animosity, or on a principle of paradox and contradiction. They have two words of detraction for each one of praise which filial pride, or any good motive prompts, and their delight is to rummage in forgotten libels. For them, the acrimonious pamphlets of past time, scraps of discreditable and hostile diaries and letters are cherished treasures. They are a fund on which they draw freely. Sometimes they forge.

Occasionally what may be described as these defamatory experiments, have gone so far and assumed a shape so precise as to require notice. This was so in one instance, within the recollection of many of my immediate fellow citizens. I refer to a series of anonymous publications as to General Reed, in the autumn of 1842, under the signature of "Valley Forge," in a Philadelphia newspaper. Though these libels were met so promptly and decisively as to force an admission that the evidence on which they rested was forgery in its most flagrant form; though the infamy of the whole affair recoiled so fatally as to destroy the paper in which the publications appeared; though falsehood was, to the eye of any historical student, palpable in every line, and the result of detection proved it to be so; there were those who read and believed it all, and applauded the agents of this dark plan of detraction. I have no doubt there are some yet who are willing to believe in what was marked with the stain of conceded fraud, and that the "Valley Forge forgeries" are carefully preserved to be revived, hereafter, to vilify anew the character of the dead, and wound the affections of the living. Two of these spurious letters were re-printed as genuine in this city, within the last three years.*

* Evening Bulletin of October 12th, 1863. The first communication of "Valley Forge" appeared on the 14th of September, the last on or about the 24th of October, 1842. The Journal ceased to exist some time during the same winter. Its Editor having in vain endeavoured to ascertain the anonymous writer who had decoyed him into this scheme of infamy, voluntarily surrendered the manuscripts to the

It is doing General Reed's contemporary enemies injustice to connect them with assailants of this description. Yet the association is not mine. But for what is known as the Cadwalader pamphlet, the slanders of a later day would have perished at their birth, it being the practice of the authors of the new coinage, whenever their spurious issue was detected, to fall back on it; and the argument always has been, that this pamphlet was genuine, and worthy of notice and reply. It is the ultimate reliance, and by an ingenious involution of the genuine and the spurious, the ends of calumny have been attained, and the character of a patriot of the Revolution, a man who filled, with honour, more high public trusts than usually are conferred on one, is whispered or clamoured away, in the city of his life and fame. To all this, it would be affectation in me to pretend indifference. I have felt it, and felt it deeply. With ample materials of vindication at hand; with a trust for the character of the dead, which seemed to press more strongly upon me as I watched from day to day the course and apparent fruition of these schemes of detraction, it has been hard to be silent. For a long while, with a determination not to be dragged, by secret and anonymous assailants, into possible controversy with the living, I was content to wait till I should be able to submit to the public a carefully digested mass of positive evidence, in the form of a biographical work, on

gentlemen whose families had been defamed, and died in May, 1845, at Washington.

which my ancestor's claim on the gratitude of his country might rest. My biography of President Reed was published in 1847, and, so far as I am able to judge, was kindly welcomed. In one respect, especially, this approval gratified me, aside from the pleasure of knowing that my labour had not been in vain to make Pennsylvania proud of one of her sons. It gratified me to find that my personal friends, and even those who were still more disinterested, approved of the moderation with which I discussed points of disputed politics; and of the absence of anything tending to give pain to a living being. I am not aware of one written word of my own, that was not in a kind spirit, and in deference to the feelings of others, and this, too, with strong temptation occasionally, to speak out painful truth, let it wound whom it might. When, in my biography, I came to the Cadwalader controversy, I thus referred to it:

"Judging from the newspapers and pamphlets, the year 1782, which found Mr. Reed a private citizen, was more convulsed by party spirit, raging apparently without restraint, than any previous period. The accredited newspaper organs of the two parties were filled with articles of extreme ferocity, directed at the respective leaders; and towards Mr. Reed especially, as one whose mere resignation of authority did not satisfy his enemies, the most intense animosity was manifested. There was no stint to anonymous defamation. On the side of the Constitutionalists quite as able partisans were in the field, using their pens offensively as well as defensively. Among them, one who wrote under the name of "Valerius," and whose identity never was clearly ascertained, attracted great attention. The main object of his assault, made with great bitterness and eloquence, was Mr. Dickinson, who in November, 1782, had been elected President by a small majority over General Potter, the Constitutional candidate. So effective did these attacks become, that Mr. Dickinson found it necessary to answer them, and to make an elaborate defence of his public conduct, in reply to this anonymous assailant. It would be entirely aside from the aim of these volumes to revive or minutely to refer to such controversies. They were in every way discreditable; they may be consigned to the oblivion which has nearly overtaken them, and may well be left for the congenial research of a class of men, happily very limited, who take a malignant pleasure in defaming the memory of our Revolutionary patriots. Occasionally, controversies of a graver kind occurred at this season of diseased excitement. Of this description was one of a very painful nature, which, in the fall of 1782, Mr Reed was involved in, with his former companion-in-arms, General John Cadwalader. Pamphlets of great acrimony were published on each side. These pamphlets are now before me, but it is most consonant with my feelings to the living and the dead, that the controversy should be dismissed with this incidental reference, which its importance at the time seemed to require, and with the expression of the conviction that had the lives of the parties, and especially of him who made the assault, been prolonged, and opportunities such as we now have, been afforded, of collating testimony, and allowing transient resentments to subside, the fierceness of the controversy would have been succeeded by far more amiable feelings. But in less than three years from its date both parties were in their graves."*

This seemed to be the best mode of treating a subject which, in some of its relations, was of great delicacy. To omit all reference to it, would have been to give colour to the idea that I was unprepared, (unwilling I certainly was,) to discuss it. To do so in detail, would be to open anew a controversy long since gone by, to excite unpleasant feelings, and possibly to affect my personal relations to those with whom I have always lived on terms of friendliness, and to whom I had no desire to give pain. To speak of it as a subject on which, time, had the lives of the parties been prolonged, might have shed a conciliatory influence, and yet, as one, as to which, if forced into controversy, I had no misgiving, seemed to be the true course. In pursuing it, I have reason to believe I had the approval of all fair-minded and considerate readers. Those only were disappointed, who

---

* Life of Reed, vol. 2, page 382. Mr. Reed died March 5th, 1785 Mr. Cadwalader, 10th February, 1786.

hoped to see the living discredited by a revival of the altercations of the dead.

No sooner, however, was the biography of President Reed given to the public—no sooner were kind words of approval heard—no sooner did it seem certain that his public character and services were, by the simple exposition of truth, about to be appreciated in Pennsylvania, and, throughout the country—no sooner were the letters of Washington, and Lafayette, and Greene, and Wayne, and Henry Lee, to Mr. Reed read, and his actual position, as their most valued and thoroughly trusted friend, illustrated by evidence, than it was thought necessary, in a sort of restless, mischief-making spirit, to try further experiments on public credulity, and to burnish up ancient weapons which had nearly rusted in their sheaths; in other words, to print and circulate the Cadwalader Pamphlet of 1783. Of its merits, I mean to speak clearly and decisively, so that about it, now, or hereafter, there shall be no misunderstanding. A single word as to its various re-publications, the first of which was in 1848. I was willing to account for this by attributing the enterprise to a mercenary motive; the cupidity of an unscrupulous publisher, who hoped, by a new edition of an ancient story, to make a few dollars. But I am constrained to believe, that it, too, was the fruit of secret and inveterate hostility, to be gratified, at any cost, and by any means; in short, that the authors of the forgeries of 1842, were again, in another form, busy at the secret work of malevolence. In this instance, they were working on genuine materials. No one questions that General Cadwalader's pamphlet is genuine, or that it involved charges by a responsible accuser. That it did great injustice, and that its allegations were groundless, having their origin in intense political animosity, and were so interpreted at the time, it will be my effort to demonstrate. The mode and number of these republications are remarkable. The first, in 1848, was printed in secret, with a preface endorsing and adopting the forgeries of 1842, and, though deposited for sale at an obscure book store, with pains taken, as the contrivers of the scheme imagined, to secure extensive circulation. The date of the preface was "Trenton, December, 1846;" in point of fact the pamphlet was printed in 1848, at Philadelphia. Why all this indirection; this falsifying of dates, had the object been a fair one?—and why, if the aim were the mere correction of a mistake of history, was it necessary to distribute secretly, thousands of advertising circulars, all carefully directed and pre-paid? Yet, this was done. It seemed as if the desire to do me and mine injustice, was not to be checked by considerations of labour or expense. One result, immediately ensued. There was an universal burst of indignation, and the faint whispers of approval, or excuse, were scarcely audible. None, I have reason to know, were more annoyed by it than General Cadwalader's descendants.

Still, the authors attained one object. They re-produced this almost forgotten pamphlet, and a number of copies were put in circulation, enough at least, to embalm a painful controversy, for future and mischievous reference.

It was again printed, with the forged documents, in 1856. I have reason to believe that a new coinage of calumny and perhaps forgery, for they have generally been associated, was suppressed, or withheld in consequence of the catastrophe of the Arctic, in 1854, and the death of my brother, Mr. Henry Reed. The sorrow, which bowed a whole family to the earth, disarmed, for a time, these secret and industrious artificers of evil.

The next revival of this ancient scandal was by Mr. John C. Hamilton, in the second volume of his "History of the Republic of the United States of America, as traced in the writings of Alexander Hamilton and his contemporaries;" a book designed, as it were, to chrystallise around the elder Hamilton, all the great results, and merits, and successes of the Revolution. Had the author of this grotesque work limited himself to the illustration of the services of his ancestor, there could have been no temptation to say a word about Mr. Reed, with whom, Mr. Alexander Hamilton had few, or no relations of any kind; but, as the theory of the book is, not merely, that Hamilton did everything, but that no one else did anything, the author in his wide circuit of disparagement, gratuitously assailed Mr. Reed. This attack was, like every one of the kind, wantonly made, and in the absence, very well known, at a vast distance on the other side of the globe, of the only person who could repel it. How it was subsequently, on one point, met, the reader may see in the correspondence in 1859, between Mr. Hamilton and me, recently published, in which he was content to rest, as he does still, under a direct charge of having fabricated the date, and imagined the contents of a letter, and of having mis-quoted one document, and mis-directed another, (New York Historical Magazine, December, 1866.) Though the main topic of Mr. Hamilton's ill-natured comment is the correspondence in 1776, with Charles Lee, like all the other purveyors of this sort of defamatory rubbish, he fell back upon the reserve of the Cadwalader pamphlet.

In 1863, it appeared again, 'by subscription,' stealthily of course, and though got up at great expense, and, printed in Albany, no place of publication, or publisher's or printer's name is to be found on its pages, and no one has been willing to acknowledge an agency in it.

The "subscription" list for this re-issue must be a curiosity, but like every thing else, it is studiously concealed. I ascertained who the three individuals were who acted as a sort of 'Committee of Publication,' but the ambush of the other 'subscribers' was perfect. This re-print is catalogued at the Franklin library of this city as 'The gift of the Publisher.' On my inquiring who this was, the librarian informed me either that he was not at liberty to say, or that the person did not wish his name known. This did not at all surprise me.

Last, in the catalogue of these resurrectionists of calumny, is Mr. George Bancroft, in the ninth volume of his History of the Revolution. I had reason to look for a different treatment of the subject at his hands, at least so far as this, that I imagined, in the apparent friendliness which existed, he would have given me an opportunity of criticism and explanation before he adduced evidence and expressed opinions so singularly hostile. But Mr. Bancroft is the judge as to his own conduct. There were indications in his eighth volume of a disposition to disparage the services of Mr. Reed, but as they were ambiguous, and the book came to me 'with the Author's regards,' I did not think it worth while to notice them. Not so, this ninth volume. It fairly bristles with calumny. Whenever, and it is quite frequently, Mr. Reed's name is alluded to, there is a sneer, or an imputation. He is a 'traitor,' (p. 229) a 'deserter,' (228) a 'coward,' (172) a 'pretender,' (106). In short he, and General Greene—the latter in a milder form—are throughout, the chief objects of Mr. Bancroft's vituperative rhetoric. I have sought in vain to account for this mischievous animosity, and am driven to attribute it to the infection of the poisonous politics of this our day, which have acidulated tempers and dispositions quite as sweet as Mr. Bancroft's and Mr. John C. Hamilton's. Be all this as it may, opinions thus expressed, and accusations so barbed, and venomous, I am compelled to notice. I shall consider them fairly. So far as they come directly within the course of my vindication, they shall be noticed in the text, and when they are aside from it, in notes. No one of these resuscitated slanders shall be intentionally omitted, and, if I use language of decision, let it be understood, there is abundant excuse in the grossness of the provocation.

That the reader may have a glimpse of the *animus* of Mr. Bancroft, and that attention may not, by and by, be diverted from the strict line of discussion, I pause here to refer to the manner in which Mr. Reed's name is introduced by him. It is an illustration of Mr. Bancroft's spirit throughout. Speaking of the negociation with Lord Howe, in 1776, with the details of which every student is familiar, Mr. Bancroft says:

"Reed, who was already thoroughly sick of the contest, thought 'the overture ought not to be rejected,' and through Robert Morris, he offered 'most cheerfully to take such a part as his situation and abilities would admit." (page 40.)

The "quotation marks" are Mr. Bancroft's, and the reader will be surprised to learn that there is no such thing in the letter from which the quotation pretends to be made. Mr. Reed neither said nor hinted that Lord Howe's overture "ought not to be rejected," nor did he offer "to take such a part" as is suggested. His language in the letter to Mr. Morris, is this: Mr. Bancroft actually mutilating the last sentence.

"If it, (the communication) can be improved in any respect, either to give time, or discover the true powers these Commissioners have, or in any other way, I shall most cheerfully take such a part as my situation and abilities will admit, and as may be directed."

As to "the rejection of the overture" Mr. Bancroft's perversion is still more flagrant. Mr. Reed says:

"The Declaration of Independence is a new and very strong objection to entering into any negociation inconsistent with that idea. But I fancy there are numbers, and some of them firm in the interests of America, who would think an overture ought not to be rejected, and, if it could be improved into a negociation which could secure the two points mentioned above, would think the blood and treasure well spent."

This is the only reference to the "overture" or its "rejection" in this letter or in any other, from first to last, and certainly is that which Mr. Bancroft alludes to. Mr. Reed adds, and, with this before him, Mr. Bancroft undertakes to say "he was thoroughly sick of the contest."

"I have no idea from any thing I have seen or can learn that if we should give the General and Admiral a full and fair hearing, the proposition would amount to any thing short of unconditional submission, but it may be worth considering whether that once known and all prospect of securing American liberty in that way being closed, it would not have a happy effect to unite us into one chosen band, resolved to be free or perish in the attempt."

This is the herald, as it were, of a series of defamatory statements, each of which I pledge myself to show to be unworthy of credit. Mr. George Bancroft has chosen to array himself with the persistent defamers of my ancestor, and has a position before the public as an ambitious writer of History, which makes it my duty to break the silence I have so long and so resolutely maintained. I propose now to reply fully to these conglomerate calumnies, and to submit such a defence of General Reed as will, I trust, put them to rest at once, and forever.

I begin of course at the "*origo mali*," the controversy of the last Century.

The Cadwalader controversy was in the year 1782-3, more than six years after the incidents in which it is supposed to have had its origin, are said to have occurred. In determining the relative attitude of the parties to this unfortunate difficulty, I have no professions of absolute impartiality to make, while I do not distrust my ability to do justice to Mr. Cadwalader, and to see defects of character, or temper, or conduct in my ancestor. With due allowance for strong filial feeling, it seems to me the subject may, without much effort, be considered in a very temperate spirit. I mean to try so to treat it.

General Cadwalader was a Philadelphian by birth, and according to the best information I have, a man of easy fortune. In the patriotic movements at the beginning of the colonial troubles, he took an active part. He, and his brother Lambert, were members of the Provincial Convention of 1775, and both held commissions in the military corps organized by Pennsylvania, in 1776. They were brave, high spirited men. Colonel Lambert Cadwalader was made prisoner at Fort Washington, and never afterwards entered active service. In the campaign of 1776, John Cadwalader commanded a Pennsylvania regiment, but was not, I believe, in the field till December of that year, when he was stationed with a body of about fifteen or eighteen hundred men, at Bristol. He remained with the army till after the battle of Princeton. In January, 1777, Washington recommended him for military promotion. In February, Congress appointed him one of the new Brigadier Generals, a post which he declined accepting, as "he conceived the war was near a conclusion." He never was regularly in service afterwards. In the winter of 1777-8 Cadwalader and Reed joined Washington, as volunteers, and were with him, counselling and aiding in the operations near Philadelphia. In December, 1777, on being offered a post in the Pennsylvania line, Cadwalader refused to accept it, and in June, or July, 1778, fought his duel with Conway. The two Philadelphia soldiers were again volunteers with Washington at Monmouth. In September, Congress, at the instance of a Committee, of which Mr. Reed was Chairman, offered Cadwalader a Cavalry command; this also, he, then residing with his family in Maryland, declined. Except a short period of service in the Maryland Legislature, he never, afterwards, was other than a private man. This is, I believe, a fair summary of General Cadwalader's services. During the greater part of the War, he resided on his estate in Maryland, occasionally visiting Philadelphia, to share in the fierce political broils which so long distracted this community.

Of Mr. Reed's career, from July 1775, when he joined Washington on his way to Cambridge, till his term of office as President of Pennsylvania ended in 1781, I do not feel it necessary to say a word. The record of his public services is before the world, and, this, certainly may be said of it, that there was not a year or a day, in which, for the public cause, he was not making some effort or sacrifice, and earning from his countrymen, and especially his fellow-soldiers, gratitude in its strongest and most sincere expression. Though, like Cadwalader, he declined Continental rank, unlike him, he thought it a duty to forego speculative objections to a frame of local government, and to take office and discharge public duty under the Constitution of Pennsylvania. When appointed Chief Justice in 1777, he declined office; when elected to the Presidency in 1778, he accepted it, and Washington "very sincerely" rejoiced. Who was right, and who wrong, no one now doubts. We know what judgment was formed and expressed by Mr. Reed's contemporaries who had a deep interest in the question; as I have said, by Washington, and by Wayne, and Greene, and Henry Lee. The student of our history will, we think, agree in the opinion which has elsewhere been expressed, that it was well for the general cause, that at the most critical periods of the war, in 1779, 1780, and 1781, when the heaviest burthens rested on the Middle Colonies, a man so full of energy, and intellectual resources, as Mr. Reed, was in Executive office in Pennsylvania. The more this period of our history is studied, the brighter will his record be. It was Pennsylvania that nobly sustained the general cause, and he was the guiding and animating spirit of her executive councils. It was a poor return for all he did and sacrificed, to be at the end, assailed by those who, while he was toiling and wearing away a feeble constitution in public service, were living in seclusion and luxury.

The year 1782 found Reed and Cadwalader private citizens. The state of local affairs I cannot better describe than I already have in the Memoir which has been given to the public. The scene was a very sad one.

On the 7th of September, 1782, there appeared in the columns of the "Independent Gazetteer," the organ of the Anti-Constitutional party of Pennsylvania, the following publication, dated the 3d.:

1. Was not General R—d, in December, 1776, (then A———t G———l of the continental army), sent by General Washington to the commanding officer at Bristol, with orders relative to a general attack, intended to be made on the enemy's post at Trenton and those below on the 25th, at night?

2. Two or three days before the intended attack did not General R—d say, in conversation with the said commanding officer,

at his quarters, that our affairs looked very desperate, and that we were only making a sacrifice of ourselves?

3. Did he not also say, that the time of General Howe's proclamation offering pardon and protection to persons who should come in before the 1st of January, 1777, was nearly expired; and that Galloway, the Allen's and others had gone over and availed themselves of the pardon and protection offered by the said proclamation?

4. Did not he, General R—d, at the same time say, that he had a family and ought to take care of them; and that he did not understand following the wretched remains of a broken army?

5. Did he not likewise say to the said commanding officer, that his brother (then a colonel or lieutenant colonel of militia) was at Burlington with his family, and that he had advised him to remain there, and if the enemy took possession of the town, to take a protection and swear allegiance? It is well for America that very few general officers have reasoned in this manner; if they had, General Howe would have made an easy conquest of the United States. And it is very obvious, that officers of high rank with such sentiments, can have no just pretensions to patriotism or public virtue; and can by no means be worthy of any post of honour or place of trust where the liberties and interests of the people are immediately concerned.

BRUTUS.

Philadelphia, September 3, 1782.

This was an anonymous publication, and no one ever avowed the authorship of it. General Cadwalader expressly disclaimed it. The newspapers of the day attribute it to Doctor Benjamin Rush, and, as he subsequently made himself a chief witness in support of the accusation against Mr. Reed, was bitterly hostile to him, and was addicted to this mode of secret assault;

there is reason for attributing to his busy pen, the initiation of this wretched controversy. The "Brutus" of 1782, after involving two gentlemen in angry dispute, never came from his ambush. So far as he is concerned, it was a stab in the dark.

Instantly, on its publication, Mr. Reed addressed a note to General Cadwalader, enquiring if he were the author, and asserting, without, however, any personal imputation, the falsehood of the hinted accusation. To this, on the 10th of September, Cadwalader replied, denying that he was "Brutus," but re-asserting the charges in a form quite as offensive. On the 11th, the following card appeared in the journals of the day:

"To the Public."

Satiated with public business, and the honours which are supposed to attend it; no candidate for office or appointment of any kind, it was my wish to live a private and peaceable citizen. But it seems the sacrifice of no small portion of my time and fortune is not sufficient, without a sacrifice of character also. A set of men in this city, uninjured and unprovoked by me, are weekly pouring forth some abuse under anonymous signatures, and in a late paper it is insinuated under a number of queries that in the year 1776 I meditated an abandonment of the cause of my country, and desertion to the enemy and communicated such intention to the commanding officer at Bristol. I do not hesitate to pronounce it an infamous falsehood, and with sincerity and upon the honour of a gentleman, solemnly declare no such conversation as alluded to in these queries ever passed, of which, I hope in a few days to exhibit the most satisfactory proof, the nature of the case admits of.

Joseph Reed.

After a sharp personal correspondence, Mr. Reed redeemed the pledge of submitting his case to the public judgment, and in November, 1782, published a pamphlet with which every historical student is familiar. It has been but once re-printed in the long interval of eighty-five years, and but for the fear of expanding this publication too much, I should be glad to re-produce it, and let an injured man, as it were from the grave, speak for himself. I am conscious of no little pride in the earnest eloquence and high literary ability of this defence. My vindication is really supplementary. In the early part of 1783, the Cadwalader pamphlet appeared in reply to Mr. Reed. Before considering it, and the evidence it is supposed to contain, as I shall do fully, and, I hope conclusively, I desire to give to the world some contemporaneous testimony, of the good and brave men of those days of trial, as to the merits of the controversy as presented by the parties themselves. I have in my possession many letters of this kind. It would extend this publication too much, were I to print them all. I therefore content myself with two—from a gallant soldier of the Revolution, him whom Washington most cherished and trusted—the Marcellus of our infant story, whose friendship for Mr. Reed, from the time they met within the lines of Cambridge, never abated nor was interrupted. With any fair-minded man, it would conclude all question as to Mr. Reed's fidelity to the cause of his country. I make extracts from the originals in my possession.

General Greene to Charles Pettit.

Charleston, April 3, 1783.

* * * I have seen Governor Reed's publication. I think it an excellent performance, and it is much admired. On almost every question, I could give the fullest confirmation, so far as my opinion can have weight. The attempt to traduce him, as having a design to go over to the enemy, is truly wicked. General Cadwalader never had such a thought. I am persuaded nothing but party rage could induce him to countenance such an insinuation. No man in America had so good an opportunity to know Governor Reed's sentiments and intentions as I had, and I know at the time they urge suspicions, he was urging the enterprise at Trenton, as he says. And as to the arguments founded upon his not taking the oaths, they are as ridiculous as they are wicked. He was opposed to the Constitution, and in hopes of getting some alterations in it was the reason why he did not take the oaths to the state. Was there not a great part of the principal men in the state in the same predicament? Their objection was not to the cause but the Constitution. It was my advice to him and General Cadwalader, both, to take up the Constitution as it was; and as the people would have more confidence in them, they might form it as they pleased. A measure of this sort would have reconciled and united all parties, and I am persuaded this was Governor Reed's intention in taking upon him the charge of government. We had frequent conversations together, to this effect. The abuse and scurrility thrown out against him, betray so much rancour and malice, that it destroys itself. He will live beloved and respected by every good man and friend to his country, in spite of all they can say to his prejudice. His good sense and natural resources will support him, when his enemies shall not dare to show their heads. * * * *

On the 23rd of April, 1783, Greene wrote directly to Mr. Reed.

Headquarters, April 23, 1783.

I thank you for the pamphlet you sent me. I had read it before, and have the pleasure to assure you it is much admired.

Everybody reads it with pleasure and conviction. I wish I had been in Philadelphia. I would have given you all the support my little influence might have had. I am better acquainted with the history of your conduct than any other person. The insinuation of your intention to desert over to the enemy is infamous, and I am sure General Cadwalader never entertained such an idea, nor would have asserted such a thing, but from the influences of party rage. Indeed; I think Philadelphia has something infatuating in its air. No character escapes abuse, and the innocent as well as the guilty are all arraigned as party or spleen directs. Good God! what will this lead to. I would sooner be an honest plowman than a public officer upon such terms.*

Again in November, 1783, months after the Cadwalader publication, when Mr. Reed visited England, Greene, standing faithfully by his ancient friend, wrote to Lafayette.

Philadelphia, *Nov.* 9, 1783.
"DEAR MARQUIS:

This will be handed you by my good friend, Governor Reed, whose merit and active zeal, you are perfectly well acquainted with. Nor, can you be ignorant of the ungenerous measures which have been taken here to lessen his public estimation. Every man who has the pleasure of his acquaintance must feel an honest indignation at the unmerited treatment he has met with; and a pleasing satisfaction that his abilities will triumph over party and faction."

To Rochambeau, and D'Estaing, he wrote in the same strain of earnest affection. Mr. Reed's infirm health

* This letter, with the exception of one passage, was published in my Life of Reed, vol. 2, page 395. The passage relating to General Cadwalader was omitted, from the feeling which, throughout, controlled me, of trying to avoid giving pain.

prevented him from visiting the continent and delivering these letters; and, for this reason, they have remained in my possession. The student of our history need not be told how valuable this voluntary testimony of General Greene is. It was his fortune to pass through the war without a reproach. He shared in the early reverses and final triumphs of the Revolution. He had, throughout, Washington's affectionate confidence. He was actively engaged in the military operations on the Delaware, in 1776, and, knowing better than any one else, Mr. Reed's conduct, at the moment when he was charged with disaffection pronounced the insinuation 'infamous.' Is it, I pause to ask, this fidelity to Mr. Reed which now attracts Mr. Bancroft's animosity to General Greene—or is it that he gained his highest laurels on fields of southern victory, and, leaving New England, sought a southern home, and died a southern man?

Greene in another letter to Mr. Reed, in 1782, said: 'The ingratitude you have been treated with by a party in Philadelphia, and by some of the officers of the army, serves but to disgust me with public life, and as a lesson of the inconstancy of human creatures. The State of South Carolina has treated me very differently. They have voted me their thanks unanimously, accompanied with a vote vesting me with an estate of 10.000 guineas. No people, I believe, ever felt a stronger impulse of gratitude. Commissioners are appointed to make the purchase. This, with the shattered remains of my little fortune, will lay the foundation for a decent support in the decline of life. The measure is new in the politics of America, and it will soon become public. Please let me know what animadversions are made upon it, particularly by the delegates and people of New England.'

What the contemporaneous public thought of these controversies may be inferred from the fact that, in the short remnant of Mr. Reed's life, his close and confidential relations with the best and purest men of our country, and especially of Pennsylvania, continued unimpaired; abroad, with Mr. Adams, and Mr. Jay, and Mr. Laurens, at home with George Bryan and Jonathan Dickinson Sergeant and Clement Biddle, and James Hutchinson, and John Bayard, and Jared Ingersoll, and especially, with William Bradford, (afterwards Washington's Attorney General,) whom Mr. Reed drew from retirement to place in high position, and who repaid the kindness by an affectionate friendship which never intermitted.

After the Cadwalader pamphlet, Mr. Reed was chosen by the Assembly of Pennsylvania to conduct, at Trenton, the Wyoming controversy, as the colleague of Mr. Bradford, Mr. Sergeant, and Mr. Wilson, and on the 16th of April, 1784, the following minute of the Assembly, attests the public estimation, in which, to the latest hour of his life, in spite of all the defamation which party fury had hurled at him, he was held. One of the sure re-actions in politics had occured, since 1782. The proscriptive 'Republicans,' such was the party name then, had been defeated at the polls, and the 'Constitutionalists' were again in the ascendant.

"Agreeably to the order of the day the house proceeded to the election of Delegates to represent the State in the Congress of the United States for the ensuing year; and the ballots being taken it appeared that the Honourable Joseph Reed, Cadwalader Morris, William Montgomery, Joseph Gardner and William Henry, of Lancaster, Esquires, were duly elected. 'I have,' wrote the Speaker of the House, 'further to express the earnest desire of the House, that you repair as soon as possible to Trenton, to meet with Congress, that this State may be represented in that honourable body."

But, as I have elsewhere said, this honour, the just reward of public service, came too late. The hand of death was upon him. In December, 1783, his will is dated, and, there, will be found the almost dying words with which he repelled these dark accusations.

"My situation in life has made me the object of much envy, calumny and reproach; I therefore, on this solemn occasion, declare that any charge of infidelity to my country, correspondence with the enemy, injustice to the State, or individuals, which has been made against me, is false. I served my country with fidelity, and usefulness, as General Washington's and General Greene's numerous letters will testify. I served Pennsylvania, in particular, to the very great injury of my family, but with equal integrity, disclaiming all offers and opportunities of serving myself. If the State will allow for the depreciation of my salary during my administration, and also £193 which I forfeited as a purchaser of a State Island lot, but which was never exacted from any other purchaser who failed in payment, I shall be obliged to it. I desire that there may be no pompous funeral, but quite plain, as nearly like those in 1776 as possible, and to be laid by my wife. If I am of consequence enough for a funeral sermon, I desire it may be preached by my old friend and instructor Mr. Duffield, in Arch street, the next Sunday after my funeral. And now I close this serious business and shall meet death with composure, having no other concern than for my children, whose interests I have too much neglected for the service of the public; however I recommend them to the care of Providence and the kindness of friends."

Mr. Reed died in March, 1785. "I never" wrote General Richard Butler, "saw so great a number of people at one funeral in America." All orders, classes and parties, united in paying him the last honours. The officers of the army; the Militia of the city; the Assembly and Executive Council, with the President, Mr. Dickinson, (once a political adversary,) with a large concourse, followed him to the grave.

It is this man, thus honoured to the last hour of his life, and thus, in death lamented, whom, I, his grandson, am called upon to vindicate against a charge of deep dishonour, suggested whilst he was living, and revived by the busy artificers of slander, eighty years after he died.

This vindication I proceed to make:

The pamphlet of 1783 contains two charges, one expressly made, and one, very directly insinuated.

1. That in December, 1776, Mr. Reed, in extreme despondency, thought of making his peace with the enemy by accepting the terms offered by their Commissioners, and, so said to General Cadwalader.

2. That, with that view, he entered into a correspondence of a treasonable character with Count Donop, the Hessian Commander of the outposts in New Jersey.

As to the first, it will be observed that the only direct evidence adduced is that of General Cadwalader himself, his double brother-in-law, Philemon Dickerson, John Nixon, and Doctor Benjamin Rush. All the others, Jacob Rush, Joseph Ellis, Davenport, Bradford, David Lenox, and Nichols, merely tell hearsay gossip—what other people told them. How little value should be attached to such testimony, will appear from a contradiction, now for the first time in print, I am able to give one of them—Mr. Bradford. Bradford's certificate, published by General Cadwalader, is this:

"These are to certify, that, in December 1776, and January 1777, I, the subscriber, was Major of the second battalion of Philadelphia Militia, whereof John Bayard was Colonel, and then lay at Bristol, and part of the time opposite Trenton, on the Pennsylvania side. That while we lay at Bristol, Joseph Reed, Esq., joined us; that, during his being there and near Trenton, he often went out for intelligence, as Colonel Bayard told me, over to Burlington, in which place the enemy frequently were; that, being absent frequently all day and all night, I as frequently enquired what could become of General Reed. Colonel Bayard often answered me, he feared, he had left us and gone over to the enemy. One time in particular, being absent two days and two nights, if not three nights, Colonel Bayard came to me with great concern, and said he was fully persuaded General Reed was gone to join the enemy and make his peace. I asked how he could possibly think so of a man who had taken so early a part and had acted steadily. He replied, he was persuaded it was so, for he knew the General thought it was all over, and that we could not stand against the enemy, and at the same time wept much. I endeavoured all I could to drive such notions from him, but he was so fully persuaded that he had left us and gone over to the enemy, that arguing about the matter was only loss of time. Colonel Bayard often making mention, that he knew his sentiments much better than I did. After being absent two or three nights, General Reed returned, and I never saw more joy expressed than was by Colonel Bayard; he declaring to me he was glad General Reed was returned, for he was fully convinced, in his own mind, that he was gone over to the enemy.*

WILLIAM BRADFORD.

March 15, 1783.

---

* Mr., or Major Bradford, who gives this certificate, was William Bradford, the elder. His two sons were Thomas, a printer and publisher, and William, Attorney General of Pennsylvania, in 1780, afterwards Judge of the Supreme Court, and at the time of his death in 1795, Attorney General of the United States in the Washington administration, Mr. Reed's intimate friend, one of the executors of his will and guardian of his children. He wrote the laudatory inscription on Mr. Reed's tombstone. In Mr. Bradford's will, now before me, dated in 1788, this passage occurs: "In remembrance of the friendship and patronage I experienced from Joseph Reed, Esquire, in his lifetime, I give and devise to such of his children, as shall be alive at the time of my decease, and to their heirs, a tract of land in Northumberland County, containing 1005 acres, granted to me by patent; also, the sum of £1000, payable in certificates, at the discretion of my executors, and the farther sum of £150, payable in one year after my decease." This, and all other of Mr. Bradford's testamentary dispositions, were rendered nugatory by the adjudication in the well known and reported case of Bradford *vs.* Boudinot, 2 *Dallas' Reports*, 266, 2 *Yeates*, 170, in which Doctor Rush was the chief witness against the wills. Mr. Thomas Bradford, who inherited, as heir at law, belonged to a different school of politics, was the intimate friend of Doctor Rush, and the printer of the Cadwalader pamphlet. He lived to a very advanced age, dying in 1837. The brothers were not on friendly terms.

Among Mr. Reed's papers I find the following affidavit, which speaks for itself, being that of a man, whose high character in public and private life is well known in this community. A more emphatic and precise denial could hardly be framed. It is dated the 5th of December, 1783—of course after the Cadwalader pamphlet appeared.

"Whereas Mr. William Bradford, Senior, heretofore a Major in the Second Battalion of Philadelphia Militia, under my command, hath, in a pamphlet published by General Cadwalader, certified that I frequently communicated to him suspicions of the fidelity of General Reed, in the winter of the year 1776, and apprehensions of his being gone to the enemy; that he despaired of the American cause, and that I knew his sentiments on the subject. I do hereby declare that I never entertained a doubt of the fidelity of General Reed, or the least suspicion of his intending to join the enemy; and further, that in the most private and intimate conversations, he never expressed to me a sentiment of that kind or discovered that despondency which would lead me to draw such a conclusion. I well remember my often expressing my concern and anxiety at his and Colonel Cox's frequent visits to Burlington, and my apprehensions that they would either be betrayed by the inhabitants or surprised and taken by the enemy. I expostulated with him on this head more than once. His answer was to me, that he knew the people and could depend upon them, and that our situation required constant and daily intelligence. My frequent mention of the uneasiness I was under on this occasion, may have been misunderstood by Major Bradford. The justice due to a much injured character has led me to give this counter certificate." JOHN BAYARD.*

* "John Bayard, chairman of the Committee of Inspection, for the County of Philadelphia, a patriot of singular purity of character and

Still, there remains what may be called the positive testimony, and to it, I direct my attention; and, first, to that of General Cadwalader himself, which it is best to give in his own words:

"I had occasion to speak with you, a few days before the intended attack on the 26th of December, 1776, and requested you to retire with me to a private room at my quarters—the business related to intelligence—a general conversation, however, soon took place concerning the state of public affairs, and after running over a number of topics;—in an agony of mind, and despair strongly expressed in your countenance and tone of voice, you spoke your apprehensions concerning the event of the contest; that our affairs looked very desperate, and we were only making a sacrifice of ourselves;—that the time of General Howe's offering pardon and protection to persons who should come in before the first of January, 1777, was nearly expired; and that Galloway, the Allens, and others, had gone over and availed themselves of the pardon and protection offered by said proclamation;—that you had a family and ought to take care of them, and that you did not understand following the wretched remains (or remnants) of a broken army; that your brother, (then Colonel, or Lieutenant Colonel of the militia—but you say of five months' men, (which is not material) was then at Burlington with his family, and that you had advised him to remain there and if the enemy took possession of the town, to take a protection and swear allegiance, and in so doing he would be perfectly justifiable."

If General Cadwalader be understood to say that in December, 1776, before the success at Trenton, Mr.

---

disinterestedness, personally brave, pensive (*sic*), earnest and devout." Bancroft, vol. 8, page 385.

Reed, in confidential intercourse with him, was despondent as to the prospects of the Americans, it is certainly not worth while to dispute it. There was despondency, deep despondency, and the highest in military rank felt it; and to their families and friends expressed it. "General Reed," says "Mr. Nixon," on my enquiring the news, and what he thought of affairs in general, said that appearances were very gloomy and unfavourable; that he was fearful *or* apprehensive the business was nearly settled, *or* the game almost up, *or* words to the same effect.* That all this, or some of it, may have been said, is quite probable, for we find that on the 18th of December, Washington wrote to his brother: "Between you and me, I think our affairs are in a very bad condition. In a word if every nerve is not strained to recruit the new army with all possible speed, I think the *game is nearly up.*" "Some effectual remedy," wrote Mr. Morris to Congress, on December 23d, "must be applied to this evil, (the depreciation of the currency) or *the game will be up;*" the very words which General Cadwalader and his friend Mr. Nixon, thought it treasonable for Mr. Reed to utter.

But General Cadwalader, in 1783, meant to say more. He meant to charge Mr. Reed with more than transient despondency, when, in 1778, angered at the prosecution

---

* In Mr. Nixon's certificate these disjunctives are all in *italics*, indicating an intense uncertainty as to what was really said.

of his friend, Mr. William Hamilton, who, with Carlisle and Roberts, was tried for high treason, he, for the first time, talked of treasonable defection. "Though living in the closest intimacy," says Mr. Clymer, "I never (before) heard you drop the most distant hint of any defection of Mr. Reed, of which, I myself, had no suspicion." He meant to charge much more than despondency, when a year later, he furnished Arnold, on his trial for official misdemeanour, of which he was convicted, and at the very time a secret traitor, with a weapon of calumny to be hurled at his prosecutor. He meant to charge cowardly disaffection, and it is this charge which must be met. It cannot be evaded. It ought not to be understated; for, while I do not condescend to ask a stricter rule of evidence, in view of the enormity of the imputed crime, I have a right to infer from the subsequent relations of the accuser and the accused, that the former did not believe a charge so gross had any foundation. There is not a trace of General Cadwalader having breathed this accusation until the Treason trials of 1778. The only attempt to show that he ever whispered it before, is in Colonel Hamilton's letter of the 14th of March, 1783, in which he says that after an effort of memory "he thinks" the matter was mentioned to him, sometime in the campaign of 1777, and, with great caution, he adds: "It is the part of candour to observe that I am not able to distinguish with certainty whether the recollection I have of these words arises from the strong impression made by your declaration at the time, or from having heard them more than once repeated within a year past."

The secret thus kept was a perilous one, to both parties. 'Mr. Reed avowed his intention to desert to the enemy at the most critical position of affairs, in terms so distinct that I was on the point of arresting him, and, this, I kept secret from all, including the Commander-in-Chief, to whom I was bound to reveal it. I kept it secret from motives of expediency and in the exercise of discretion which I considered advantageous.' This, almost in terms, is what General Cadwalader said two, or three, or seven years after. And this being so, may we not ask, why was it ever told? Why was it put in circulation in 1778, or in 1779, or in 1782, gloomy and critical periods of our story? Why was it kept back till party asperities and political bitterness called it forth? Why was it talked of in coffee houses and clubs, as General Cadwalader tries to prove it was? Why was it blurted out in anger on the trial of a cause when Mr. Reed was merely discharging a professional duty? And why was it, at last, "conveyed" as a weapon of offence to a man like Arnold, and, brandished in the light of day by a mercenary, jobbing traitor? Does not it look as if it might have been an after thought, and that if General Cadwalader, in 1783, believed what he said, it was through some peculiar mental process which clouds the memory and makes an angry man think he remembers what never occurred. It is not the first time and will not be the last, when men have chafed themselves into delusions.

Arnold's language on his trial in January, 1780, was this:

"Conscious of my own innocence, and the unworthy methods taken to injure me, I can with boldness say to my persecutors in general, and to the chief of them in particular, that in the hour of danger, when the affairs of America wore a gloomy aspect, when our illustrious General was retreating through New Jersey with a handful of men, I did not propose to my associates basely to quit the General and sacrifice the cause of my country to my personal safety, by going over to the enemy and making my peace."

Mr. Reed, in his pamphlet of 1782, says: "When Arnold's insinuation dropped, a smile of contempt manifested itself throughout the room." And Mr. Sparks well remarks: "The boastfulness and malignity of these declarations are obvious enough, but their consummate hypocrisy can be understood only by knowing the fact, that, at the moment they were uttered, Arnold had been eight months in secret correspondence with the enemy, and was prepared, if not resolved, when the first opportunity should offer to desert and betray his country. No suspicions of such a purpose being entertained, these effusions were regarded as the offspring of vanity, and the natural acerbity of his temper. They now afford a remarkable evidence of the duplicity of his character, and of the art with which he concealed the blackest schemes of wickedness under the guise of pretended virtue and boast of immaculate innocence."*

And now, simply hinting incidentally these general reasons for incredulity, I proceed to show that it was an after thought, and that, in December 1776, General Cadwalader did not think Mr. Reed unfaithful to his country, a traitor in heart, in his own words, "a base man who had once raised his foot to take a step" that ought to have consigned him to the scaffold. This is plain language, for, as I have said, I do not desire to understate anything on the part of the accuser.

Let me recall the reader's attention to the familiar story of those hours of trial. There is no precision in General Cadwalader's dates. The perilous conversation, he says, took place "a few days before the intended attack, on the 26th of December, 1776." Doctor Rush, the other witness, fixes the date of his conversation "a few days" before the battle of Trenton, though, as he says, it occurred on a ride to "Headquarters near New-

---

*Life and Treason of Arnold, page 141. "If,' wrote Washington to Reed on the 20th of November, 1780, 'if Arnold, by the words in his letter to his wife,' 'I am treated with the greatest politeness by General Washington and the officers of the Army, who bitterly execrate Mr. Reed and the Council, for their villainous attempt to injure me,' 'meant to comprehend me in the latter part of the expression, he asserted an absolute falsehood."

town," it must have been before the 18th, for, then, "Headquarters were near the Falls of Trenton." It is to be presumed that the pretended date was within the eight or ten days before the 26th of December, and so I shall consider it, in the view I desire to present of Cadwalader's relations to Reed, when, and after this secret infamy was said to be revealed.

They were at Bristol, with a small body of militia and a few Continental troops; the enemy in unknown force in front, on the eastern side of the Delaware; a small body of Americans under Griffin, at or near Mount Holly; Washington about ten miles above, meditating an attack; and Philadelphia, panic-stricken and disaffected below. Then it was that Washington communicated to Reed and Cadwalader, the details of his proposed attack. "For Heaven's sake," said he, writing to Reed, "keep this to yourself, as the discovery may prove fatal to us." Cadwalader and Reed had concerted a plan to cross and attack the enemy below. The plans were considered by them in confidence. Nay more, when the lower one was relinquished, it was agreed that Mr. Reed should cross the river and confer with Griffin, then in actual contact with the enemy. This was done; the companion of the errand, as he has been, of unmerited calumny, being Colonel John Cox. This critical duty was performed, and the fact ascertained that no assistance could be expected in that quarter, and that Griffin was falling back. Then it was, that further confidence was reposed in Mr. Reed by his fellow-soldier, Cadwalader. No one but they knew Washington's secret. He had trusted them, and they, each other, and for fear of accidental disclosure, Mr. Reed went to Philadelphia to hurry on reinforcements. He returned, just in time to take part in the unsuccessful attempt to pass the Delaware at Dunk's Ferry on the night of the 25th, and was one of the few officers who did cross and with Colonel Cowperthwaite remained on the other side.* He returned to Bristol on the morning of the 26th, before news of Washington's success came and, when it was known, took part in the movement above Bristol on the 27th. And here, I venture to interrupt this line of thought by an incidental illustration of the failures of General Cadwalader's memory on matters of fact. The troops at Bristol crossed the Delaware on the 27th, it being supposed that Washington was still on the left bank. On landing, it was ascertained that he had re-crossed,

---

* Mr. Bancroft says: 'Sending back word that it was impossible to carry out their share in Washington's plan, Reed deserted the party and rode to safe quarters within the enemies lines at Burlington, having previously obtained leave for a conference with Donop.' Vol. 9, p. 229.

It would be difficult to compress in few words more gross misrepresentation than there is here. The impossibility of crossing was patent to every body after the first experiment. Mr. Reed did not 'desert' in any sense. His contemporary enemies never said he did. He was accompanied by another officer of rank whose fidelity never was suspected. Burlington was not within the enemy's lines, and Mr. Reed returned to Bristol before any news was received from Trenton. Of the Donop fiction, I shall speak hereafter. I incidentally annotate this illustration of Mr. Bancroft's persistent tendency to misstatement.

and it became a question what should be done by the force below.

Writing of this, in 1783, General Cadwalader, in his pamphlet, says: that on the receipt of news that Washington had re-crossed, "Colonel Hitchcock proposed returning to Bristol, *I instantly declared my determination against it*, and recommended an attack on Mount Holly, as, from the information we had of the force there, we might easily carry it."

There now lies before me a certified copy from the State Department of a letter from General Cadwalader to Washington, dated on the very day of the occurrence, 'Burlington, ten o'clock, 27th,' in which he says:

"As I did not hear from you this morning, and being prepared to embark, I concluded you was still on this side, and therefore embarked and landed about 1500 men about two miles above Bristol. After a considerable number were landed, I had information from the paymaster of Colonel Hitchcock's brigade, that you had crossed over from Trenton. This defeated the scheme of joining your army. We were never more embarrassed which way to proceed. *I thought it most prudent to retreat*, but Colonel Reed was of opinion that we might safely proceed to Burlington, and recommended it warmly, lest it should have a bad effect on the militia, who were twice disappointed. The landing in open daylight must have alarmed the enemy, and we might have been cut off by all their force collected to this place. We had intelligence immediately afterwards, that the enemy had left the Black Horse and Mount Holly. Upon this we determined to proceed to Burlington. Colonel Reed and two other officers went on from one post to another till they came to Bordentown, where they found the coast clear. Colonel Reed and Colonel Cox are now there, and we shall march at four to-morrow morning for that place."

Again, there is an illustration of mistaken memory, when, in reply to the statement in Mr. Reed's address, that he went to Burlington before day but did not leave Dunk's Ferry 'till he saw the last man re-embarked,' General Cadwalader in his pamphlet of 1783, said, this could not be, for 'there is no circumstance better ascertained than that many of the men were not brought back till *eight o'clock* the next morning.' Writing to General Washington, on the very day, (25th) Cadwalader said: "We concluded to withdraw the troops that had passed, but could not effect it till near *four o'clock* in the morning. The whole was then ordered to march back to Bristol." Four o'clock on Christmas morning is certainly long "before day."

Thus closed this chapter of unreserved confidence, for it is not necessary for vindication to pursue the narrative, and scrutinizing it from first to last, from the day when at Washington's request or suggestion, Mr. Reed joined Cadwalader at Bristol, till they pursued the flying enemy to Bordentown, it seems to me difficult, from this unquestioned record of mutual faith and active co-operation, to resist the conclusion that the whole phantom, of Mr. Reed's disaffection, was the coinage of passion, and what General Greene called "party rage." "General Cadwalader never could have had such a thought."

Before adducing further proof on this point, for it is abundant, I pause on a matter of painful interest connected with these events; painful in this: that General Reed, thus in his lifetime assailed, went to his grave without recovering what would have been conclusive on the question he was forced to discuss. Time, however, has in this respect done justice. Instantly on the publication of the anonymous queries of September, 1782, Mr. Reed wrote to Washington, saying: "My memory suggests to me a letter I wrote your excellency from Bristol containing reasons for an attack on the enemy; if that letter can be obtained, I am persuaded it contains sentiments of a very different nature from those of which I complain, and would be particularly useful." Washington replied that "being in the field perfectly light," he had no papers with him, public or private, and could not therefore furnish the letter, expressing, at the same time, his disbelief of the charge understood to be made. Nor was it ever recovered during Mr. Reed's lifetime; nor indeed, for fifty years after his death, when Mr. Sparks found it in the Department of State, and printed it in the appendix to the fourth volume of the Works of Washington. There, for the first time I saw it.

Reed to Washington.

Bristol, December 22, 1776.

Dear Sir:

Pomroy, whom I sent by your order to go to Amboy, and so through the Jerseys and round by Princeton to you, returned to

Burlington yesterday. He went to South Amboy, but was not able to get over; upon which he came to Brunswick—passed on to Princeton, and was prevented from going to Pennington, upon which he returned to Burlington by way of Cranbury. His intelligence is, that he saw no troops, baggage wagons, or artillery, going to New York, except about eight wagons, which he understood had the baggage of some of the light horse, who had been relieved and were going into quarters. At Cranbury he saw sixteen wagons going down to South Amboy, for the baggage of about five hundred men, who were to quarter about Cranbury, being enlisted forces commanded by one Lawrence. At Brunswick, he saw four pieces of cannon; the number of men he could not learn, but they did not exceed six or eight hundred. Princeton, he says, was called head-quarters, and there he saw a very considerable body of troops coming out of the college, meeting house and other places where they quartered. He understood they were settled in their winter quarters, and had given over further operations till the spring. In Burlington County, he found them scattered through all the farmers' houses, eight, ten, twelve and fifteen in a house, and rambling over the whole country.

Colonel Griffin has advanced up the Jersey's with six hundred men as far as Mount Holly, within seven miles of their head-quarters at the Black Horse. He has written over here for two pieces of artillery and two or three hundred volunteers, as he expected an attack very soon. The spirits of the militia here are very high; they are all for supporting him. Colonel Cadwalader and the gentlemen here all agree, that they should be indulged. We can either give him a strong reinforcement, or make a separate attack; the latter bids fairest for producing the greatest and best effects. It is therefore determined to make all possible preparation to-day; and no event happening to change our measures, the main body here will cross the river to-morrow morning, and attack their post between this and the Black Horse, proceeding from thence, either to the Black Horse or the square, where about two hundred men are posted, as things shall turn out with Griffin. If they should not attack Griffin as he expects, it is probable both our parties may advance to the Black Horse, should success attend the intermediate attempt. If they should collect their force and march against Griffin, our attack will have the best effects in preventing their sending troops on that errand, or breaking up their quarters and coming in upon their rear, which we must endeavour to do in order to free Griffin. We are all of opinion, my dear General, that something must be attempted, to revive our expiring credit, give our cause some degree of reputation, and prevent a total depreciation of the continental money, which is coming on very fast; that even a failure cannot be more fatal than to remain in our present situation; in short, some enterprise must be undertaken in our present circumstances, or we must give up the cause. In a little time the Continental army will be dissolved. The militia must be taken before their spirits and patience are exhausted; and the scattered, divided state of the enemy affords us a fair opportunity of trying what our men will do, when called to an offensive attack. Will it not be possible, my dear General, for your troops, or such part of them as can act with advantage, to make a diversion, or something more, at or about Trenton? The greater the alarm, the more likely that success will attend the attacks. If we could possess ourselves again of New Jersey, or any considerable part of it, the effects would be greater than if we had never left it.

Allow me to hope that you will consult your own good judgment and spirit, and not let the goodness of your heart subject you to the influence of opinions from men in every respect your inferiors. Something must be done before the sixty days expire which the Commissioners have allowed; for however many affect to despise it, it is evident that a very serious attention is paid to it, and I am confident that unless some more favourable appearance attends our arms and cause before that time, a very great number of the militia officers here will follow the example of those of Jersey, and take benefit from it. I will not disguise my own sentiments, that our cause is desperate and hopeless, if we do not take the opportunity of the collection of troops at present, to strike some stroke. Our affairs are hastening fast to ruin, if we do not retrieve them by some happy event. Delay with us is now equal to a total defeat. Be not deceived, my dear General, with small, flattering appearances; we must not suffer ourselves to be lulled into security and inaction, because the enemy does not cross the river. It is but a reprieve, the execution is more certain, for I am very clear, that they can and will cross the river, in spite of any opposition we can give them.

Pardon the freedom I have used. The love of my country, a wife and four children in the enemy's hands, the respect and attachment I have to you, the ruin and poverty that must attend me, and thousands of others will plead my excuse for so much freedom. I am, with the greatest respect and regard, dear sir, Your obedient and affectionate humble servant.

JOSEPH REED.*

---

* Here again I stoop to pick up another of Mr. Bancroft's poisonous shafts. He says: "The elaborate letter of Reed to Washington, December 22, 1776, proves, at most, that Reed was not in the secret. As Adjutant General, his place was at Washington's side, if he was eager for action." Mr. Bancroft knows perfectly well that Reed was on detached duty at Bristol by Washington's orders. But he does not content himself with this mild slander. He goes on to say: "Lord Bacon says: 'Letters are good when it may serve afterwards for a man's justification to produce his own letter.' In 1782, Reed wished to produce this letter for his own justification, &c." If such was Mr. Reed's design in writing this letter, he would have kept a copy to produce on a fit occasion and this we know he certainly did not. As I have said in the text, he never saw this letter during his life. A part of it was printed by Gordon in 1788, three years after Mr. Reed's death. I have no words with which to characterize Mr. Bancroft's treatment of these subjects. He seems to revel in defamation of certain individuals, and if the reader will turn to another of Lord Bacon's Essays, that on 'Truth,' (*Whately's edition, page* 2) he may see what mixture it is that gives zest to this enjoyment. I never claimed for Mr. Reed any very large share of merit in what he then did and said and wrote, but, even that, Mr. Bancroft begrudges.

This letter and others to be quoted by and by, tell the whole story. They are the letters of an anxious and resolute man; of one who sees the future clearly and states his views precisely. They are the letters of a suggestive, enterprising man, capable of exertions; whom the gloom of the probable future did not incapacitate. The letter of the 22d, was written within the "few days" of suspense before the affair at Trenton. Yet this letter, no one of the busy men who, from time to time, have been disinterring these buried controversies has had the honesty to re-print.

Thus was Mr. Reed regarded and confided in during the campaign of 1776 by General Cadwalader himself, and though, by the certificate of Hamilton, an attempt is made to show that in 1777 he declared his distrust, and spoke of the imputed infidelity of the year before; yet the fact is incontestable that, throughout that year, in all the operations in the neigbourhood of Philadelphia, Cadwalader and Reed were acting together on terms of the most affectionate confidence. It was their common honour to be recommended in the same letter by Washington, for military promotion. "I shall take the liberty," he wrote to Congress, "of recommending Colonel Cadwalader as one of the first of the new appointments. I have found him a man of ability, a good disciplinarian, firm in his principles and of intrepid bravery. I also beg leave to recommend Colonel Reed to the command of the horse, as a person in my opinion in every way

qualified; for he is extremely active and enterprising, many signal proofs of which he has given this campaign."*
They served together from Germantown to Monmouth.

If General Cadwalader in 1777, did intimate to Hamilton this more than suspicion of his companion in arms, it must have been, we are bound to suppose, in no spirit of wanton and gratuitous disparagement, but from some sense of public duty, Hamilton being in close connection with the Commander-in-Chief. What then, on this theory, can be thought of the following letters to Mr. Reed the two from Washington being re-produced to show that then, as ever, he reposed in Mr. Reed the most implicit confidence? It was more than an appearance of trust. It was affectionate and abiding faith. One of them I now publish for the first time, for it was recovered after the appearance of my Memoir in 1847.

WASHINGTON TO REED.
Middlebrook, June 23, 1777.

DEAR SIR:

Your favours of the 12th and 18th inst. are both before me, and on two accounts have given me (*illegible*); first, because I much wished to see you at the head of the Cavalry; and secondly, by refusing of it, my arrangements have been a good deal disconcerted. As your reasons for refusing the appointment, are no doubt satisfactory to yourself, and your determination fixed, it is unnecessary to enter upon a discussion of the point. I can only add, I wish it had been otherwise, especially as I flatter myself that my last would convince you that you still held

---

* Sparks Washington IV. 292.

the same place in my affection that you ever did. If inclination or a desire of rendering those aids to the service which your abilities enable you to do should lead you to the camp, it is unnecessary for me I hope to add that I should be extremely happy in seeing you one of my Family whilst you remain in it.

The late coalition of parties in Pennsylvania is a most fortunate circumstance; that, and the spirited manner in which the militia of this State turned out upon the late manœuvre of the enemy, have in my opinion given a greater shock to the enemy than any event which has happened in the course of this dispute because it was altogether unexpected and gave the decisive stroke to their enterprise on Philadelphia. The hint you have given respecting the compliment due the Executive powers of Pennsylvania I thank you for, but can assure you I gave General Mifflin no direction respecting the militia, that I did not conceive, nay that I had not been told by Congress he was vested with before; for you must know that General Mifflin, at the particular instance and by a resolve of Congress had been detained from his duty in this camp near a month to be in readiness to have out the militia, if occasion should require it, and only got here the day before I received such intelligence as convinced me that the enemy were upon the point of moving; in consequence of which, I requested him to return and without defining his duty desired he would use his utmost endeavours to carry the designed operation into effect, conceiving that a previous plan had been laid down by Congress on the State of Pennsylvania so far as respected the mode of drawing the militia out. The action of them afterwards, circumstances alone could direct. I did not pretend to give any order about it.

It gives me pleasure to learn from your letter that the reasons assigned by me to General Arnold for not attacking the enemy in their situation between the Raritan and Millstone met with the approbation of those who were acquainted with them. We have some among us, and I dare say Generals, who wish to make themselves popular at the expense of others or who think the cause is not to be advanced otherwise than by fighting; the peculiar circumstances under which it is to be done and the consequences which may follow are objects too trivial for their attention; but as I have one great end in view, I shall, maugre all the (*illegible*) of this kind, steadily pursue means which in my judgment lead to the accomplishment of it, not doubting but that the candid part of mankind, if they are convinced of my integrity, will make proper allowance for my inexperience and frailties. I will agree to be loaded with all the obloquy they can bestow if I commit a wilful error.

If General Howe has not manœuvered much deeper than most people seem disposed to think him capable of, his army is absolutely gone, if panic-struck, but as I cannot persuade myself with a belief of the latter, notwithstanding it is the prevailing opinion of my officers, I cannot say that the move I am about to make towards Amboy accords altogether with my opinion, not that I am under any other apprehension than that of being obliged to lose ground again, which would indeed be no small misfortune, as the spirits of our troops and the country are greatly revived (and I presume) the enemy's not a little depressed by their late retrograde motions.

By some late accounts, I fancy the British Grenadiers got a pretty severe peppering yesterday, by Morgan's rifle corps; they fought, it seems, a considerable time within the distance of from twenty to forty yards and from concurring accounts of several of the officers more than one hundred of them must have fallen.* Had there not been some mistake in point of time for

*Mr. Bancroft has no sympathy with Virginia, and sometimes shows it in an odd way. Speaking of Morgan, a most gallant soldier, but of whose freaks at Elizabethtown Point, Mr. Bancroft gives a most remarkable account, he says: "Next to Washington, Morgan was the best officer whom Virginia sent into the field, though she raises no statue to the incomparable leader of her light troops." (page 131.) To what soldier of the Revolution has Massachusetts, or New York, or Pennsylvania raised a statue? There are hideous Penns and awkward Franklins, and Hancocks, and Otis, and Websters, and Storys, and Everetts, and Horace Manns, but there is no Monumental stone for

marching the several brigades that were ordered upon that service, and particularly in delivering an order to General Varnum, I believe the rear of General Howe's troops might have been a little rougher handled than they were, or if an Express who went to General Maxwell the evening before, had reached him in time to co-operate upon the enemy's flank, for which purpose he was sent down the day before with a respectable force, very good consequences might have resulted from it; however it is too late to remedy those mistakes now, and my paper tells me I can add no more than to assure you, that I am Dear Sir,

Y'r affect'e.
Go. Washington.

Cadwalader to Reed.

Head Quarters, 30th *November*, 1777.

Dear Sir:

We were consulting about winter quarters when your letter came to hand, and I detained your servant in hopes of giving you their determination, but the General has required the opinion of the officers in writing, at 10 o'clock to-morrow morning. I showed your letter to the General. Many of the officers are for going into winter quarters, on the line from Lancaster towards Easton. If this is attempted, I am sure the troops will march there only to be disappointed. By the best information, those towns are crowded with inhabitants from the city and little shelter can be found there.

The General officers will set the example of going home, the field officers will follow their example: captains and subalterns will expect the same indulgence and the soldiers will apply for furloughs; and if refused will desert. By these means the army

the ancient soldiers of the North. It may too admit of a question, and, that without disparagement, whether Morgan was a better officer than Henry Lee, who was a Virginian. Morgan was born in New Jersey.

will be dispersed through the different colonies and it will be impossible to collect them in time to open an early campaign. The country on every side will be left to be plundered and vast numbers will apply for protection. The inhabitants will be dispirited, the credit of our money ruined, the recruiting service at an end and inevitable ruin must follow. It has been proposed to take post at Wilmington and the little towns in that neighbourhood and build huts for those who cannot be provided with quarters. If we do not do this, the enemy may take possession of this post with two thousand men or three, which they can easily spare and by this means secure the lower counties on the eastern shore. By taking possession of this strong post, and bringing down the gondolas, we may annoy the navigation, and by being on the spot in spring, take such measures as may oblige the enemy to come out and attack us in the field. We have good information that Cornwallis is returned and that the enemy had orders to march at two o'clock yesterday morning. The orders were not given out 'till dusk—the officers were driving about in great confusion and were heard to complain that the orders came out so late. The weather prevented, or we should certainly have had a brush yesterday. Greene and the detachment from New Jersey are all arrived in camp. We are now in full force and in perfect readiness for them, and wish nothing more earnestly than to see them out. This weather will probably delay the matter for a few days, but I have no doubt they intend us a visit or else this is given out to cover a design of making a large foraging party to New Jersey, as a great number of boats have been collected. The last seems very probable. The Marquis, you know, was in Jersey; he commanded the detachment of riflemen about 150, and 130 militia, with which he attacked a Hessian picket, 350 men, and drove them above a mile, and at dusk remained master of the field, finding a number of dead and taking fourteen prisoners. 'Tis said they lost twenty killed; we lost but three or four men. The Marquis behaved with great bravery and extols the riflemen and militia to the skies. The enemy crossed at Gloucester, covered by their shipping, and took with them about four hundred head of cattle, chiefly milch cows and young cattle. Greene intended to attack Cornwallis and had made his disposition, but prudently declined it. The attempt in my opinion was dangerous, as 2 or 3000 men could have been thrown in his rear, or a reinforcement sent over to Gloucester in the night, without his notice. Nothing more worth notice.

Cannot you come here to-morrow and advise? You can think of the matter to night. My compliments to the ladies.

Your most obedient and
Very humble servant,

To General Reed. John Cadwalader.

Washington to Reed.

Whitemarsh, December 2, 1777.

Dear Sir,

If you can with any convenience, let me see you to day, I shall be thankful for it. I am about fixing the winter cantonments of the army, and find so many and such capital objections to each mode proposed, that I am exceedingly embarrassed, not only by advice given me, but in my own judgment and should be very glad of your sentiments on the matter without loss of time. In hopes of seeing you I shall only add, that from Reading to Lancaster, inclusively, is the general sentiment, whilst Wilmington and its vicinity, have powerful advocates. This, however, is mentioned under the rose; for I am convinced in my own opinion, that if the enemy believed we had this place in contemplation they would possess themselves of it immediately. I am very sincerely, dear sir

Yours affectionately,

General Reed. G. Washington.

Cadwalader to Reed.

Head Quarters, December 10, 1777.

Dear Sir:

If I have in the least degree contributed to promote the general cause, I shall think my time well spent; as soon as the army is fixed for the winter, I shall return to my family in Maryland; but think it my duty to render every service in my power at the opening of the next campaign. I am sorry I cannot think as you do with respect to the accepting an appointment in this State; I look upon the present powers established as a most daring, dangerous usurpation; and can never consent to support or even countenance it. I opposed it as long as those engaged appeared in earnest, and as long as measures which must certainly have succeeded, were supported. The same reasons which induced the gentlemen who have given up the cause to defer the opposition till the present troubles were over, will have as much weight when the States are tired out with a long and expensive war as I conceive this government can never be changed without another revolution.

Your country is much indebted for your services and nothing is more reasonable than to repair your loss. I shall most chearfully take the first opportunity of mentioning it to the General and if it cannot be done in this line, will write to some of the members of Congress. The army marches to morrow very early.

For God's sake endeavour to suppress this dangerous faction before it gets too great a length! If it succeeds, America is lost.

I am, Dear Sir, with great respect and esteem,
your most obedient and humble servant,

GENERAL REED.   JOHN CADWALADER.

Conclusive as are these letters that General Cadwalader could not have believed in 1776 or 1777 what he alleged so positively in 1778 and 1783, it would be unjust to Mr. Reed to rest his vindication on them alone.

The accusation of 1783 was a sweeping one, and involved others besides Mr. Reed. Two gentlemen were especially assailed—Mr. Bowes Reed, (the General's brother) and Colonel John Cox, of New Jersey—the former directly, the latter indirectly.

"He (General Reed) said:"—this is the 'Brutus' charge—"that his brother, then Colonel or Lieutenant Colonel of the militia was at Burlington with his family; that he had advised him to remain there; and if the enemy took possession of the town, to take a protection and swear allegiance and in so doing he would be perfectly justified."

Mr. Bowes Reed who many years survived his brother promptly met the charge, as it was first presented by 'Brutus,' and to this contradiction it should be remembered Cadwalader's pamphlet makes no reply.

"Bowes Reed, Esquire, Secretary of the State of New Jersey, and heretofore a lieutenant colonel in the new levies of said State, being duly sworn, deposeth and saith: that, in the month of December, 1776, this deponent's time being expired in the five months' service, he returned, in bad health, to Burlington, in New Jersey, the place of his former residence, which, though not occupied by the troops of either party, was subject to the incursions of both; that during that time this deponent's brother, then Adjutant General of the Continental army, frequently came over from Bristol, where the Pennsylvania militia then lay, in order to procure intelligence of the movements and designs of the enemy, then lying at Bordentown, the Black Horse, and Mount Holly; that this deponent assisted his brother in said service by procuring and equipping spies to go within the enemy's lines, and communicating the advice occasionally received; and this deponent farther saith: that during the said time or at any other his brother never intimated to this deponent in the most distant manner any advice or encouragement to seek protection of the enemy; but on the other hand, that he was too much exposed to the incursions of the enemy and wished him to remove to a place of greater safety; and this deponent further saith: that during the said time, his said brother never expressed to him any apprehensions of the success of the cause, but seemed wholly engaged in procuring intelligence, and pursuing other methods to annoy and defeat the designs of the enemy; this deponent farther says: that his said brother, to his knowledge or belief, was not engaged in any other measure, than as above mentioned, except, that at the request of a number of the people of Burlington, who were greatly distressed by parties from each army, he publicly sent a message to Count Donop, who then commanded the troops on the part of the enemy, proposing, mutually, to keep the said parties out of the town, on which Count Donop sent a messenger with an answer, as this deponent was then informed, who returned without delivering it, as his said brother was then gone into Pennsylvania; that in a few days afterwards the surprise of the Hessians, at Trenton, took place, and the war was entirely removed from this part of the country; and farther, the deponent saith not.

Sworn before me, the 23rd day of October, 1782.

BOWES REED.

SAM. HOW.

The other individual indirectly attacked by General Cadwalader and his friends was Colonel John Cox of New Jersey. To his numerous descendants I leave the duty of doing justice to his memory, should it, in the waste of reputation which now prevails, be further assailed, merely saying that he was a man of high personal character, a sterling patriot from first to last, a gallant soldier and a most accomplished gentleman. He was one of the two who were associated with Greene when in 1778 he accepted the post of Quartermaster General. In fact, General Greene made this association the condition of undertaking so arduous and thankless a duty. With Mr. Reed, Colonel Cox was closely connected. The correspondence in my possession amply attests this. In the operations on the Delaware in December 1776, they acted together. Jerseymen by birth and education, and thoroughly familiar with the neighbourhood where the military operations were, they were associated in various perilous enterprises. Colonel Cox accompanied Mr. Reed on his visit to Griffin at Mount Holly on the night of the 24th of December, and their families were fugitives together on the edge of the pine forests. Mr. Cox shares some of the calumnies which had their origin in these scenes of trial and peril; for in the last libellous re-issue—the Philadelphia one of 1863—he is spoken of as "Reed's *particeps criminis.*" During his life, however, no one ventured openly to attack him.

The instant Mr. Reed was assailed in Oswald's paper, Colonel Cox came to the rescue of his friend, and, as early as October 20th, 1782, made the following statement, which shows the confidential relations of the parties.

CERTIFICATE FROM THE HON. JOHN COX, ESQUIRE, VICE PRESIDENT OF NEW JERSEY.

These are to certify, that, in the month of December, 1776, the subscriber, being then lieutenant colonel of the second battalion of Philadelphia militia, lying at Bristol, Mr. Joseph Reed, the then adjutant general of the Continental army, came down to the militia by the direction of the commander in chief (as the subscriber understood) that he quartered in the same house with the subscriber and was engaged in procuring intelligence from the enemy, and in the most confidential communications of the operations of the army; that the subscriber accompanied him in one to Mount Holly to Colonel Griffin and, as the subscriber understood, was treated with the most unreserved confidence both at Bristol and elsewhere with respect to the movements and designs of the troops; that his advice and opinion appeared to be much depended on, particularly with respect to crossing over and remaining in New Jersey, which led to the successes at Princeton and the favorable issue of the campaign; that the subscriber verily believes those communications to have been made at such times and under such circumstances as must have subjected the troops to certain destruction and the commanding officer to the highest censure, if, on the one hand, the person entrusted had proved unfaithful, or on the other, the commanding officer had reason to suspect him. The subscriber also well remembers that the enemy were not far distant from where we landed; that it was proposed by several officers to return to Pennsylvania; that Mr. Reed was of opinion that re-crossing the river would greatly dispirit the troops and therefore was against it, and offered to explore the country where the enemy was supposed to be; which, by the request of General Cadwalader, he accordingly did without any covering party or company, save Colonel Cowperthwaite, the subscriber, and a guide; that during the continuance of the militia at Bristol, the subscriber was on terms of the most unreserved intimacy with Mr. Reed, and had frequent confidential conversations with him on the state of affairs, which then wore the darkest appearance, in all which the said Mr. Reed never intimated, nor had the subscriber the least reason to suspect he had any intention of abandoning the cause or arms of his country to join those of the enemy; that it appeared to the subscriber, that General Cadwalader during his stay at Bristol depended in a great measure for intelligence on the said Mr. Reed and the subscriber, which their knowledge of the country enabled them to obtain for him daily; that the subscriber had frequent conversations with the said Mr. Reed during the time of our greatest difficulty and distress, in none of which did it ever appear to be the intention of Mr. Reed to abandon the cause of his country by joining the enemy, but, on the contrary, showed every disposition to oppose and counteract them and the subscriber verily believes that had any such intention been formed by the said Mr. Reed, he would have communicated it to the subscriber; that he never heard from General Cadwalader of his entertaining any doubt of Mr. Reed's attachment to or perseverance in the cause of America, or any opinion expressed by him that induced a belief that said Cadwalader entertained other than a favourable one touching the said Reed's zeal or activity in the public service.

Trenton, October 20, 1782.   JOHN COX.

Of this complete denial, General Cadwalader took no notice, for, while he referred injuriously to a relatively humble man Mr. Ellis, no word of contradiction or insinuation was levelled at Colonel Cox. That Mr. Cox was disposed to resent any disparagement of his integrity or fidelity to his country, is apparent from the following extract of a letter to Mr. Pettit, (the original now in my possession,) dated at his country place near Trenton, April 14th, 1783. It has never before been in print:

"I observe by Bradford's last paper, that Cadwalader's reply to General Reed's remarks is published. I want much to see it though I disregard anything that he or any of his toad-eaters can say with truth touching my character, and great as they may be, should they have asserted what is false, I will make them answer for their audacity."

I have said, Cadwalader made no direct reference to Mr. Cox. If, however, as has been lately suggested, Colonel Cox was the officer who accompanied Mr. Reed to Burlington, there is a remote allusion to him as the companion of a guilty errand. It is however very obscure and would scarcely be worth noticing, but for an apparent confirmation in an entry in what is known as "Margaret Morris' Journal," which has lately been disinterred, where Colonel Cox's name is introduced. Of this, I have only to say that the dates disprove the whole story. Those who think that the character of brave men can be blasted in history by an old or young woman repeating what was told by a household female domestic—black or white—I can hardly hope to convince. But that this trash has more than once, and lately (1863) been re-printed; that it is kindred in some respects to the graver libels I have been considering and that I desire to trample out even the minute varieties of the species, I should not notice it even to this extent. General Cadwalader's statement having been fairly examined and, I hope, disposed of, I turn to the extrinsic evidence he adduced on the single point—for to it I now confine myself—of Mr. Reed's 'dangerous despondency' of December, 1776.

The three witnesses are Mr. Philemon Dickinson, Mr. John Nixon, and Doctor Benjamin Rush. I have noticed Mr. Nixon's statement, and scarcely think it worth while to refer to Mr. Dickinson's, which is simply that Mr. Reed addressed to him a remark he regarded as offensive.

Dr. Rush is the witness in chief. His testimony dated in March, 1783, may be thus stated:

That in friendly and accidental conversation, on a ride to Headquarters, Mr. Reed spoke with great respect of the bravery of the British troops and with great contempt of the cowardice of the Americans, and more especially of the New England troops. He denounced 'with an oath' Mr. John Dickinson, the author of the Farmer's Letters, who, it was rumoured, for slander was very busy then, had deserted to the enemy, as having begun an opposition which we have not strength to finish. He said that a gentlemen who had submitted to the enemy had acted properly, and that a man who had a family did right to take care of them.

Such are the substantive averments, with Doctor Rush's gloss that the whole conversation indicated a great despair of the American cause, and the addition, that he repeated what he heard to his brother Jacob Rush and to John Adams, who, he gravely says, replied: "That the powers of the human mind are combined together in a variety of ways."

If Doctor Rush is to be regarded as a witness in support of a charge made by another, the obvious comment on this testimony is that it is utterly destitute of precision, except in the imprecation put into Mr. Reed's mouth when speaking of Mr. Dickinson; that it was a distant recollection, through seven long years of civil war with all its disturbing elements, and that, as in the case of General Cadwalader, it was not seriously regarded at the time, since "it did not diminish the respect" of the witness for Mr. Reed. To the suggestion of the lapse of time, it may be replied that it was Doctor Rush's habit, (as is well known,) to keep a diary or note book in which he registered all the irritating occurrences of his restless life in order that his memory even of the remote past might be kept fresh, and his resentments never allowed to cool.* This is true, and I and every other inquirer must await the time when the diary, worthless as it may be, shall be given to the world, and its supposed revelations can be scrutinized. If, in December, 1776, or at any time before 1782, Doctor Rush noted a conversation of this kind with Mr. Reed, let the entry in the diary be produced and it shall be fairly met. As Mr. Bancroft quotes this diary, perhaps, he can vouch it. If he has it and it contains any disparagement of Mr. Reed, he surely would have quoted it. I have no idea that he has it, though he so ostentatiously cites it. Nor is the story credible that Rush, on the 23d, 'saw' Washington

* *In Swift's Journal to Stella, September* 9, 1710, is this passage: "For an hour and a half we talked treason heartily against the Whigs, their baseness and ingratitude. And I am come home rolling resentments in my mind, and forming schemes of revenge, full of which, having written down some parts, I go to bed."

write the watchword 'Victory or Death!' The 23d was the day when the Commander-in-Chief wrote his confidential letter to Reed, in which he said: "For heaven's sake keep this to yourself as the discovery may prove fatal to us;" and it is not credible that he would tell a military secret to a tattler like Doctor Rush, or publish it by a watchword, or even determine on a countersign so long in advance. The whole thing don't sound like Washington, except perhaps in Mr. Bancroft's ears.*

But if Doctor Rush be "Brutus," and this, on the evidence, is my belief; if it was he who started this wretched controversy, then, his relation to the whole affair is widely different. If Doctor Rush was "Brutus," it is very clear that so far as he is concerned, the *allegata* and *probata* strangely conflict; for the "Queries of Brutus" and the certificate of Rush do not refer to the same facts or similar facts in any single point of resemblance. Why, one may ask, this discrepancy, the agents or authors being the same? Was it that, one accusation

* The only other reference in print to this Diary or Note Book is in a letter from Mr. Adams to Doctor Rush, dated 18th April, 1790, showing that it runs over many years. He says: "How many follies and indiscreet speeches do your minutes in your Note Book bring to my recollection, which I had forgotten forever! Alas! I fear I am not yet much more prudent. Your character of Mr. Paine is very well, and very just. To the accusation against me, which you have recorded in your Note Book of the 17th March last, I plead not guilty. I deny all attachment to monarchy, and I deny that I have changed my principles since 1776." (*Adams' Works, Vol. IX., page* 566.) It was a saying of John Randolph of Roanoke, that he "not only never kept a diary, but he did not like to keep company with any man who did."

being made anonymously, another was purposely held back to be used as a sort of corroboration? Why was it, "Brutus" being Rush, that the Queries referred to what Mr. Reed is reputed to have said to "the commanding officer at Bristol," and not at all to what he said to the companion of the ride to Newtown? If Doctor Rush was "Brutus," or indeed if he were only "Brutus's" chief authority, then the question directly presents itself, and shall be frankly considered—Was he a credible witness? I think, I can demonstrate he was not.

The career of Doctor Benjamin Rush, aside from his professional merits, of which I am utterly unfit to judge was that of a busy, restless, indirect man, emphatically, a man of animosities. There is not a scandal or offensive truth of the Revolution within the sphere of his action and influence that did not take wing from his tongue or pen. He was a fisher in troubled waters and upon him fell, in later life, a fearful retribution in the fierce invectives of William Cobbett,—the Rush-Light, and Peter Porcupine. The poisoned cup came back with new venom infused.

In November, 1776, Rush, described by Mr. Bancroft as one of 'the best of the whigs,' co-operated with Mr. Dickinson, whom he had recently, in private, denounced, in vehement opposition to the new Constitution of Pennsylvania. On or about the 21st December, within a day or two of the date of his pretended conversation with

Mr. Reed, he wrote to Richard Henry Lee from Bristol: "Since the captivity of General Lee a distrust has crept in among the troops of the abilities of some of our Generals, high in command. They expect nothing now from Heaven-born and book-taught Generals.* I hope in our next promotions we shall disregard seniority." There is no mistaking this allusion to Washington. Still later in the same year, Doctor Rush was with the army, and, on hearing that his father-in-law (Mr. Stockton) was a prisoner and had been maltreated, he wrote to a friend in the following strain of ludicrous exaggeration: "Every particle of my blood is electrified by revenge and if justice cannot be done in any other way, I declare I will, in defiance of the authority of Congress and the power of the army, drive the first rascally Tory I meet with, a hundred miles barefoot through the first deep snow that falls in our country * * * * 'I long to be satiated with revenge at the Scotch Englishmen—Hyder Ali,' (the Nana Sahib of those days,) 'is the standing toast of my dinner table."† In 1777, he was at Princeton and is said to have recorded in his dreary Note Book that General Mercer did not die of his wounds, but from natural causes. In March 1778, for the work of secret accusation of some body never seemed to intermit, General Washington wrote to Congress: "Enclosed

---

* Doctor Rush either caught the phrase "Heaven-born Generals" from his friend Charles Lee, or gave it to him. Bancroft Vol. 9, page 207.
† Letter of Rush to R. H. Lee, December 30, 1776.

you have a copy of a letter, which I received a few days ago from Doctor Rush. As this letter contains charges of a very heinous nature against the Director General, Doctor Shippen, for mal-practices and neglect in his department, I could not but look upon it as meant for a public accusation and have therefore thought it incumbent on me to lay it before Congress. I have showed it to Doctor Shippen, that he may be prepared to vindicate his character if called upon. He tells me, Doctor Rush made charges of a private nature before a Committee of Congress appointed to hear them, which he could not support. If so, Congress will not have further occasion to trouble themselves in the matter."

But Doctor Rush hunted higher game than Medical Directors. In the winter and early spring of 1778, when Congress was squabbling at Yorktown, and Washington and his wretched soldiers were suffering at Valley Forge, Patrick Henry, then Governor of Virginia, received at Williamsburg an anonymous letter, in which this passage occurred:

"The Northern army has shown us what Americans are capable of doing with a General at their head. The spirit of the Southern army is no ways inferior to the spirit of the Northern. A Gates, a Lee, or a Conway, would in a few weeks render them an irresistible body of men. The last of the above officers has accepted the new office of Inspector General of our army, in order to reform abuses; but the remedy is only a palliative one. In one of his letters to a friend he says: 'A great and good God hath decreed America to be free, or the General and weak counsellors would have ruined her long ago.' You may rest assured of each of the facts related in this letter. The author of it is one of your Philadelphia friends. A hint of his name, if found out by the handwriting, must not be mentioned to your most intimate friend. Even the letter must be thrown in the fire. But some of its contents ought to be made public in order to awaken, enlighten and alarm our country—I rely upon your prudence."

What is dignified by this anonymous assailant, as 'prudence,' sympathy with a correspondent willing to wound and yet afraid to strike, was no part of the noble Virginian's nature. He did not recognise his "Philadelphia friend" by "the handwriting." He did not "throw the letter into the fire," but forwarded it at once to Washington, with this comment: "While you face the armed enemies of our liberty in the field, and by the favour of God have been kept unhurt, I trust your country will never harbour in her bosom the miscreant who would ruin her best supporter. I wish not to flatter; but when arts unworthy honest men are used to defame and traduce you, I think it not amiss, but a duty, to assure you of that estimation, in which the public hold you." Washington's answer was prompt and decisive. "The anonymous letter with which you were pleased to favour me was written by Doctor Rush, so far as I can judge from a similitude of hands. This man has been elaborate and studied in his professions of regard for me; and long since the letter to you." * * * * * * * "This is not the only insidious attempt that has been made to wound my reputation. There have been others equally base, cruel, and ungenerous."

In 1779, Doctor Rush was an active participant in the heated, local politics of Pennsylvania, a contributor to the newspapers, and took part with General Cadwalader in the tumultuous town meetings of that dreary year, having for their main object the embarrassment of Mr. Reed's Executive Administration. It was the year of "Fort Wilson," and its bloody incidents. Then, too, he resumed his congenial work of anonymous scribbling. On the 24th of October, 1779, he wrote signing it "an old friend" to Charles Lee—a moody, discontented and disgraced man, who hated Washington and Reed with equal intensity: "Have patience; time and posterity will do you justice. The summer flies that now din our ears, must soon retire. Nothing but virtue and real abilities will finally pass muster, when the public cool a little from the ferment into which the great and sudden events of the late Revolution have thrown us. I would rather be one of your dogs in a future history of the present war, than possess the first honours that are now current in America, with the characters which I know some of our great men merit. Poor Pennsylvania has become the most miserable spot on the surface of the globe." In 1781, Doctor Rush with the fluency which his animosities stimulated wrote to Gates, (also under a cloud and discontented) as to his fears of a monarchy and aristocracy from those whom he describes as "the Sachems of the Potomac and the Hudson" meaning Washington whom he hated, and, probably, the Livingstons and Schuylers. And so it continued to the bitter end, for we find that Doctor Rush's antipathy to Washington if not to his friends long survived the exasperations of war. "Doctor Rush tells me," says Mr. Jefferson in his 'Ana' of twenty years later, (the 1st of February 1800,) exactly forty days after Washington died amidst the tears of a whole people with the exception of a few who felt as did Doctor Rush—"he (Rush,) tells me that he had it from Asa Green, that when the Clergy addressed General Washington on his departure from the Government, it was observed in their consultation that he had never on any occasion said a word to the public which showed a belief in the Christian religion, and they thought they should so pen their address as to force him at length to declare publicly whether he was a Christian or not. They did so. However, he observed, *the old fox was too cunning for them.* He answered every article of their address, except that, which he passed over without notice."

It was this writer of anonymous defamation, this vehement partisan, he, who could stand on Washington's fresh grave, and scoff at the great inhabitant below; it was he who was Mr. Reed's chief assailant in 1782 and 1783, who, in all probability, initiated the controversy and who certainly volunteered to be a chief witness. Hence, the reader will see the relevancy to the questions

I have been considering, of this analysis of Doctor Rush's character. As a witness for anything in which his passions were involved, I have a right to describe him as utterly unworthy of belief. That he was especially hostile to Mr. Reed has already been stated, and will not be disputed. The mysterious diary, if it ever sees the day, will, I doubt not, be a new revelation of this hatred, which did not abate so long as its object was among living men. I have recently seen an ancient newspaper which throws some light on the special ground of this antipathy, affecting not only Doctor Rush, but his brother and co-witness, Mr. Jacob Rush. It is the Freemans' Journal of Wednesday, March 9, 1785, four days after Mr. Reed's death. It contains a statement by Mr. Sergeant, who had been Attorney General of Pennsylvania in the early part of Mr. Reed's Administration, as to the circumstances under which Mr. Jacob Rush had become an unsuccessful applicant for office to President Reed. Mr. Sergeant thus describes the experiment and its results:

"Mr. Rush desired me barely to mention his name, as Attorney General; not wishing to make a point of it or to urge it; but merely to signify his willingness to accept, in case of an appointment." * * * * * * "I was determined to acquit myself of my promise, and waited on the President (Mr. Reed) to let him know that I was in hopes they had provided themselves with an Attorney General; and that, if so, I had drawn my last indictment. He was polite enough to ask me if I had thought of a proper person. Hitherto I had mentioned no one. I named Mr. Rush. The President roared out in a peal of laughter, and for some time would not believe me in earnest. I told him what had passed, hinted that I did not apprehend the matter to be new to him, and intimated that the government might acquire some new friends by the measure. He said that he had no objection to the obliging Doctor Rush and his brother; though they very little deserved any favour at his hands from their treatment of the friends of the Constitution, but his objection was that Mr. Rush was not equal to the task. The lawyers on the other side, (I forget the expression but I believe it was the Tory lawyers,) will run him down and make him contemptible and us ridiculous. Besides, he has not patience for the drudgery of the office; and the first difficult business he meets with he will fly in a passion and fling a resignation in our faces. He will not hold the office two months. Recollect sir, the man who recommends another to office, ought to be answerable for him. Will you vouch for Mr. Rush? Will you be answerable for his abilities; for his steadiness?' I really thought that by this time I had sufficiently done my errand; so far as to intimate that Mr. Rush was willing to accept the office of Attorney General. I went no further. We agreed to drop the subject to say nothing of it to any one—and this is the first time that I have ever fully explained it. It was no very agreeable answer to give to Mr. Rush, and he never asked an explanation. It was perhaps best as it was." * * * * * "Mr. Reed, I know had no desire of hearing more on the subject, and I am sure I had none; for I must confess that I felt foolish enough in doing the errand, which made the President's laughing at me the more sensibly felt."

These, then, are the disappointed and exasperated men who became Mr. Reed's accusers in 1782. Sustained as his vindication is by the concurrent testimony of Washington, and Greene, and Bayard, and Cox, honoured as he was to the end of his life, by his fellow-citizens, his fellow-soldiers, and the Legislature of his State, I have a right on this or any other point of controversy to assume that he cannot be condemned on the uncorroborated testimony of two of his most embittered political opponents. There are, I repeat, no other witnesses on this point against him. This chapter of calumny is closed.

Having, I hope, candidly collated the testimony on the point of the alleged conversation of December, 1776, and shown how utterly untrustworthy it is, I proceed to consider the other specific accusation—the correspondence with Count Donop.

This, also, I should prefer giving in General Cadwalader's language, but it is not easy to do so, for it is so vaguely stated and floats so indistinctly through his pages that it eludes the attempt to embody it in words. It is rather insinuated than asserted. In substance, however, it is far more grave than the one I have been considering—as much more so as an overt act of treason is than a whisper of timidity in the ear of a friend. It was this, and I shall not understate it:—"that in December, 1776, when Count Donop, the commander of the Hessian advanced guard, was at or near Bordentown, Mr. Reed sent an application for protection, for himself, his property, and 'an intimate friend,' and that this matter of protection, (thus rather hinted than clearly stated) was the subject of correspondence and negotiation afterwards, continuing until the reverse at Trenton, and Donop's retreat. This, I think, is a fair statement of it. It would be doing General Cadwalader injustice, to say that this accusation originated with him. It certainly did not, but being made by others, it was introduced into his pamphlet as a make-weight, cumulative evidence of Mr. Reed's imputed criminality. I think I have it in my power to show its exact parentage, and that it, too, had its source in personal and political animosity. To make the matter intelligible, and to show it had attracted Mr. Reed's attention before General Cadwalader assumed the paternity of it, I will here quote his account of the transaction as given in the original pamphlet. He says: "As intelligence was of the utmost importance both to General Washington and to ourselves, in conjunction with Colonel Cox of New Jersey, every exertion in our power was made to procure it: This we were enabled to effect through the medium of some persons of Burlington with whom our residence had formed an interest. In the course of this business it was necessary to pass frequently to that place. On one of these occasions the inhabitants applied to me for relief from the incursions of our troops, especially the galleymen, who distressed them without affording an advantage to us. As the Hessian patrols came daily to town, I observed it would be difficult and hardly reasonable to restrain our troops, unless the enemy would submit to the like restrictions. It was then suggested that such a proposition should be made to Count Donop, who commanded the British and Hessian troops; and I wrote a few unsealed lines to that effect, which an inhabitant of Burlington undertook to deliver. The whole transaction was of a public nature, and in the presence of several gentlemen who had accompanied me from Bristol. The bearer of my letter found Count Donop on his march to the Black Horse, and brought back an open letter mentioning that circumstance, and that as soon as his situation would admit, he would appoint a place of conference on the proposition. Having thus far complied with the desire of the inhabitants of Burlington, who chiefly are of a peaceable quiet character, and from their inoffensive conduct, as well as the services we were daily receiving from some of them, entitled to this office of kindness, I returned to Bristol. But that I may close this transaction, without interrupting my narrative of events, I shall here observe, that I was informed a flag came into Burlington a few days after, with an open letter from Count Donop, appointing a place of conference, which was sent over to Bristol and delivered to General Cadwalader in my absence. The tide of American fortune soon after turned; Count Donop retreated to Brunswick and I never saw or heard from him afterwards."

From this, as well as a reference in Margaret Morris' Diary, I incline to the belief that in it as in the other calumny Colonel Cox was implicated, and that he was "the intimate friend" so darkly alluded to in this part of the Cadwalader pamphlet. He had, and I believe Mr. Reed had not, extensive property in New Jersey within the enemy's lines, and was closely associated in these errands of peril. These being the counter allegations, one of a deep plot of secret treason and correspondence with the enemy; the other, of an open negotiation for the protection of helpless non-combatants; let us see what are the proofs adduced. The evidence on what I may call the side of the accusation, it will be observed is purely hearsay. No human being of his own knowledge can say a word. It is traced indirectly to one individual, Mr. Robert Lenox, a commissary in the British service, who gives no testimony, but who is reported to have communicated the story to his brother, Mr. David Lenox, who in turn furnished it to General Cadwalader. The certificate is dated March, 1783, four months after the Provisional Treaty had been signed, and when, one would think, there was no insuperable difficulty in procuring the direct evidence from New York, where then and for many years afterwards Mr. Robert Lenox lived. Perhaps however at a time when the wounds and passions of war were fresh, it was perilous to call as a witness against a patriot soldier "a Deputy Commissary of Prisoners under the British king." It was better to rely on the second-hand testimony of Mr., or as he was better known even within my recollection, Major Lenox, who held some military rank in the American service.

The testimony was thus hearsay without excuse or necessity. Mr. Robert Lenox never testified directly, and I am glad to note this, because he was a gentlemen of high character and unquestioned integrity. That Mr. David Lenox was a man of violent passions and, like Doctor Rush and most of those who came forward to testify against Mr. Reed, a bitter partisan of what was known as the Anti-Constitutional party, is well known in this community. I infer that he, too, had a personal grievance, from an entry that I find in the minutes of the Executive Council for 1779.

PRESIDENT REED TO CHIEF JUSTICE MCKEAN.

Council Chamber, *August* 10, 1779.

SIR:

We have been just informed that David Lenox has grossly insulted Robert Smith, Esq., one of the agents of the forfeited estates, in the execution of his office. We request you to take the most vigorous measures on this occasion, as not only the honour, but the interest of the State is deeply concerned. It being our full intention to vindicate not only the officers of the Government, but support them with our utmost weight and influence. We are also informed that one Captain Nichols, or Nicholson, a Continental officer had a share in the affray. If it should prove so, we trust some other notice will be taken of his conduct, besides that of the ordinary course of justice.

I am sir, with due respect,
Your obedient humble servant,

JOSEPH REED,
President.*

---

* Pennsylvania Archives, 1778-9, page 637, 328. This "Nichols" was probably the Francis Nichols of the Cadwalader pamphlet.

Six months after this, it seems Mr. David Lenox "obtained permission for an interview with his brother at Elizabethtown," and there "was alarmed" by the information of Mr. Reed's application to Count Donop four years before. He returned to Philadelphia and used this story as a weapon of offence against Mr. Reed, then President. "I thought it my duty" says he in his certificate, "to mention it publicly to prevent further power being put in the hands of a man who would make a bad use of it." In his own language he 'propagated' it. The fruit of this ineffectual gossip was, that in June of the same year (1780) Mr. Reed with his Council was invested by the Assembly with what were then considered Dictatorial powers, the authority to declare martial law, and in the autumn he was elected for the third time President of the Executive Council of Pennsylvania. In May, 1781, Mr. Robert Lenox came into the Delaware with a flag of truce. It was a time of great and peculiar peril. The embers of the mutiny of the Pennsylvania line were not cool. The enemy was vigilant and active everywhere. The affairs of the States, and especially of Pennsylvania were apparently desperate. There was not a dollar in the Treasury to pay ordinary expenses. Emissaries were engaged in schemes of assassination, President Reed being one of the designated victims.* Precautionary measures were necessary, and

---

* Governor Livingston's letter, 11 April, 1781.

Mr. Robert Lenox was refused permission to visit Philadelphia and was kept "for four weeks on board ship nine miles below the City." Here, again, it seems the Donop story was repeated, with the same intimation of an unknown associate of crime. Still, it produced no effect, and gained no credit. In the interval, Arnold, who was Mr. Reed's first open accuser, had become a confessed traitor, and no one seemed willing to use the weapons he had tried. After a careful search through the newspapers of the time, which, until our day, have had no rivals in ferocity, I do not find a trace of this fiction. It was no doubt to whispers of this form of calumny Mr. Reed referred in his pamphlet, in the passage which I have quoted.*

This then is the whole evidence, with the exception of Mr. Bancroft's Hessian diary presently to be noticed: the repetition by heated and prejudiced men of what they supposed had been told them years before, by an avowed enemy, an officer in the Royal Army. On the other

---

* It may have been with reference to this specific accusation—the David Lenox gossip—that Mr. Reed wrote to General Greene in June 1781. "After all, and after repeated, gross and illiberal attacks of every kind from weakness to treason, for great pains have been taken to prove me in the interests of the enemy, I am still in good health and spirits, not disgusted with the service of my country though ready to give place to any man who can serve it better. The body of the people continue my friends because they believe that I am, as I truly am, theirs; of this I have given the most unequivocal proof, because I have consented to watch for three years that others might sleep—to be poor that they might grow rich." 2d *Life of Reed*, page 360.

hand, putting aside all suggestions of inherent improbability in a charge "so fathered and so husbanded," I beg the candid reader's attention to the direct testimony on which the averment rests, that Mr. Reed's written intercourse with Count Donop was an innocent and legitimate intercession for the poor people of Burlington.

In the first place, there is the testimony of the person who carried Mr. Reed's letter to the Hessian Head-Quarters, which cannot be impaired by General Cadwalader's unsustained assertion that he was a disaffected man. If he were so, he would not have been disqualified for the errand. If he were so, he might naturally enough seek to make peace for himself, and as naturally seek to implicate Mr. Reed and his unknown friend. Mr. Ellis survived the Revolution and held positions of dignity under the new government. This is his positive, and as I have said, to this hour, uncontradicted statement:

AFFIDAVIT BY DANIEL ELLIS, ESQ., FORMERLY HIGH SHERIFF AND ONE OF THE JUDGES OF THE COURT OF COMMON PLEAS FOR BURLINGTON.

State of New Jersey, Burlington County, ss.

PERSONALLY came and appeared before me, the subscriber, one of the Justices of the Peace in the said county, assigned to keep, &c. Daniel Ellis, of the City of Burlington, Esq., a person to me well known and worthy of good credit, who being duly sworn on the Holy Evangelists of Almighty God, deposeth and saith: That some time in the month of December, in the year of our Lord, one thousand seven hundred and seventy-six, the Philadelphia militia lying at Bristol, the gallies in the river, and the Hessians under Count Donop at Bordentown and the Black Horse; the town of Burlington was much distressed by small parties coming in and committing excesses on the inhabitants; that Joseph Reed, Esq., then Adjutant General of the Continental Army, being occasionally in town was applied to by some of the inhabitants, as this deponent understood, to procure them some relief, and particularly to restrain the galley men and militia from coming into the town; that in order to effect this it was necessary that the enemy's parties should be equally restrained, and the said Mr. Reed agreed to write a letter to the Count Donop to that effect; that this deponent went to the office of James Kinsey, Esq., where the said General Reed was with Colonel Shee of Philadelphia; that several of the inhabitants were also present; that the said Joseph Reed asked this deponent if his son would carry a letter to Count Donop for the above purpose; to which this deponent replied, that if it was for the relief of the town he would go himself; upon which a letter was immediately writ; that this deponent went the next morning with the letter (which to the best of this deponent's remembrance was unsealed) and delivered the same to Count Donop, who soon after returned an answer in writing, which this deponent understood from the said Count Donop was to appoint a place for a conference upon the subject, which letter this deponent delivered to the said General Reed, (the said Mr. Reed and Colonel Shee waiting for his return); that some few days after an officer came to Burlington with a flag, with a letter from Count Donop to the said General Reed; that the people of Burlington being anxious to effect the business, exerted themselves to get the said letter over the river, (the river being then full of ice); that upon getting over they found that General Reed was at Philadelphia, so that the said officer did not see him, nor did any intercourse pass between them to this deponent's knowledge or belief; that this transaction was of public notoriety, and as this deponent verily believes, calculated for the sole relief of the inhabitants of said town, then much distressed by the irregularity of the troops and galley men, who came into the town under various pretences and plundered and ill treated the inhabitants. And further this deponent saith not.

DANIEL ELLIS.

Sworn before me, the 23d day
of October, 1783.

SAM HOW.*

I have said that, in adopting and re-producing this Donop calumny, General Cadwalader deals with it vaguely as if he was not quite sure of the ground he was treading or of the weapon that had been put in his hands. The nearest approach to precision is this interrogative imputation: "Is it not more than probable that at the interview you proposed under cover of serving the inhabitants of Burlington you intended to confer with Count Donop upon the subject of your own interest and personal safety?" Here, the insinuation is clear enough and I so accept it; and now shall show by evidence under General Cadwalader's own hand, not known to Mr. Reed when he published his pamphlet, that he was perfectly well acquainted with the object of the proposed conference, and that the letter which Count Donop wrote came to General Cadwalader and was answered by him.

* A friend in New Jersey, Mr. James W. Wall, a Senator of the United States, of whom I made inquiry as to Mr. Ellis, writes to me: "Daniel Ellis spoken of in the Cadwalader pamphlet, by whom your grandfather sent the letter to Count Donop with a flag, was not disaffected, but, on the contrary, he assisted the cause of the Colonies and was in consultation with the patriots. He was a man of considerable landed estate, which, of course would have been confiscated if he had been what Cadwalader describes; but he was in full enjoyment of it up to the day of his death, long after the close of the Revolutionary War."

Before doing so, let me refer to another matter incidentally. When it is sought to disparage my ancestor, the Diary of Margaret Morris is cited as authentic even when she chronicles the babble of her servant girls. I desire to refer the reader to it now for another purpose; as the record of what passed under her own observation, at a period when her perceptions were quickened by all sorts of anxieties, and when she bore willing testimony to the kind offices of those with whom—as her diary proves—she had no other sympathies. Recalling the Donop accusation and Mr. Reed's reply, it should be remembered that this diary never saw the light 'till fifty years after the accuser and the accused were in their graves. It will be found completely to sustain Mr. Reed.

On the 25th of December is the entry which is material to the question of the real relations to Count Donop. It is as follows:

"December 25th. An officer said to be gone to Bristol, from the Count de Nope, with a flag, and offers of letting our town remain a neutral post. General Reed at Philadelphia. An express sent to him, and we hear he is to meet the Count to-morrow at Jno. Antrim's and settle the preliminaries.

December 26th. Very stormy; we fear General Reed will not meet the Count to-day. A great number of flat-bottom boats gone up the river; we cannot learn where they are going to.

December 27th. A letter from General Reed to his brother, informing him that Washington had had an engagement with the regulars on the 25th, early in the morning, taking them by surprise; killed 50 and took 900 prisoners—the loss on our side not known—not suffered to be public."

The letter of Donop, thus by a flag publicly forwarded to Bristol was, as Mr. Reed in his pamphlet assumed, put into General Cadwalader's hands and answered by him. A copy of the answer, in Cadwalader's handwriting, (open to the inspection of any one who has a right to ask for it) is in my possession. It is in these words:

"*Bristol, December* 25, 1776.

Sir,

As Colonel Reed is not at this post at present, I opened the letter addressed to him. There is no other person here so fully acquainted with the business he proposed mentioning to you at the interview he requested. I expect he will return to-morrow morning to this post, and he will then request you to name another time and place which may be convenient to you. I did not receive the flag to-day till half past 10, A. M.

I am Sir, &c., &c.

To Colonel Donop."   John Cadwalader.

General Cadwalader in 1783, when he adopted the hearsay accusation of Mr. David Lenox, must have forgotten his own letter of 1776 to Count Donop, to which no other construction can be given than that the writer knew the negotiations to be innocent.

Among Mr. Reed's manuscripts, I find the rough draught of an Address after the recovery of this letter. It shows an intention to make another appeal to the public, and incidentally refers to the Cadwalader pamphlet as the joint production of Doctor Benjamin Rush,

Dr. William Smith, (Provost of the College and an inveterate enemy of Mr. Reed) and General Cadwalader. This intention was never carried out, and my conviction, from a careful study of everything within my reach connected with this affair, not to speak again of the honours and marks of public and private confidence afterwards conferred, is, that in its day and generation, this attack on Mr. Reed was completely abortive. Nor should it be forgotten that, in the long interval of nearly a century since the Revolution, no historical or biographical writer, English or American, friend or enemy, with one exception, ever has alluded to it. Neither Gordon—certainly no friend—nor Stedman, a loyalist, anxious to discover flaws in any American's reputation—nor Graydon, nor Ramsay, nor Marshall, nor Adams, nor Sparks, nor Washington Irving, nor Lord Mahon, nor any one ever found a trace of evidence in support of this wretched accusation, or if they did, condescended to stoop and follow it. Mr. Galloway and the fugitive loyalists, examined in Parliament in 1779, made no allusion to it.

Writing to me on kindred topics, as far back as 1842, Mr. Sparks said:

"I can say with perfect sincerity and truth, that in my examination of documents and papers relating to the Revolution, I have seen nothing that could give countenance to charges against General Reed. There is surely nothing to this effect in Washington's papers, or in those of other general officers which have come under my inspection. He had a slight difference with the Commander-in-chief in 1776, but this was of short duration, and it was after this event that Washington offered him the command of the Cavalry; and he often consulted him on military affairs, particularly in regard to the State of Pennsylvania. He was appointed a Brigadier General by Congress, and was chosen a member of that body from his native state. During a large part of the winter at Valley Forge he was present in camp, as one of a Committee from Congress for re-organizing the army; and he afterwards held the office of President of Pennsylvania, and continued in the public service till near the end of the war. Are we now to form so low an opinion of the sagacity and wisdom of the leaders of that day as to believe that they would sustain in such responsible stations a man whose patriotism they suspected, and least of all a man whom they looked upon as an enemy in disguise? The thing is so incredible in itself that it requires the strongest positive proof to clothe it with even a shadow of probability; for we cannot fix so dark a stain upon the memory of General Reed without seriously implicating the character of the eminent patriots who gave him their support and confidence.

In the public offices in London I have examined all the correspondence between the British officers in America, and the Ministers, during the war. I have no remembrance of seeing General Reed's name mentioned in these papers on any occasion."

Mr. Bancroft wrote from London in 1848:

"In looking through the archives here which have been opened to me with great liberality I have looked for traces of your grandfather but as yet have found nothing of much importance. If I do, I shall communicate it to you."

He has, it seems, been more successful since, but he had to go to the shameful records of Brunswick and Hesse Cassel, to the diaries and note books of mercenary strangers, ignorant of the English language—'Ewalds' and 'Bourmeisters' and even *Munchausens* (p.211) before he succeeded in finding what he seems to have craved so eagerly. I throw into a note a characteristic comment on Hessian testimony and Hessian conduct, from the pen of a friend of Mr. Bancroft, one who stands high on the canon of New England.*

I have spoken of an exception, I mean in English. In the year 1787—two years after Mr. Reed's death, there was published in London a pamphlet entitled "Remarks on the Travels of the Marquis de Chastellux

---

* "The Baroness de Riedesel was a lady deserving all credit when she tells what she has seen though she may have put a wrong construction upon it. But the case is not exactly the same as to everything which she may have heard. Perhaps she did not understand English perfectly well. She was the wife of a person engaged in one of the most nefarious occupations that human mind and muscle can be put to. He and his, had no quarrel with us and ours, but he had been let out for hire by the wretch called Elector of Hesse Cassel to come hither and make our wives and children widows and fatherless. If he could come on such a business, it was very fit that his wife should come with him. Heaven knows he stood enough in need of every solace of domestic love. He failed in what he came for. He sold his own blood and not ours. We caught him and his attendant reptiles and drew their fangs. If women whose husbands, fathers, sons, he would have butchered, perhaps had butchered, spat on the ground in sign of anger as his wife passed, it was a very unfeminine, discourteous, indecent act, though it was evidently an affront designed for him rather than for her; and something may perhaps be pardoned to the rage of those against whom injuries so enormous, so wicked, being committed because God's providence and man's valor dashed the miscreants to the earth in the flush of their abominable enterprise. Hired stabbers as long as they were in arms—house thieves as soon as they were beaten, they had nothing better to claim at the hands of meekness itself than mere forbearance and humanity." *North American Review*, *July*, 1852.

in North America." There is some slight reason to believe that the author of this was either General Arnold, or some mercenary writer whom he had suborned. The slander, there, assumes a form, on which I have no other comment to make, than that it is the accusation of an anonymous assailant whose testimony is the loosest hearsay, and, if it has any direct application, affects a man, Mr. Bowes Reed, who, so far as my knowledge extends, maintained throughout a long life, extending beyond the agitations and asperities of Revolutionary times, an unimpeached character. This writer, whoever he was, says:

"I join in the Marquis de Chastellux's observations on Mr. Reed. I know in the prosperous situation of the British affairs in 1777, (*sic*) and before the unhappy event at Trenton, that Bowes Reed, a brother of Governor Reed, crossed the Delaware from Pennsylvania and took with the prescribed forms a British protection from a Hessian officer, I believe Colonel Donop, at the same time, he requested one for his brother, the Governor, which Colonel Donop declined giving him unless he should appear in person. Soon after, Bowes Reed acted, himself, in a civil employment in the State of New Jersey; and the Governor, it is well known, as the Marquis observes, "published and exaggerated the offers that were made him by Governor Johnson, and attained his end of playing a leading part in the country." pp. 29, 30.*

---

* I first heard of this form of calumny from my friend, Mr. George H. Moore, of New York, who was kind enough to send me the extract I have quoted, a copy of the pamphlet being in the Astor Library. In this pamphlet, Washington is thus spoken of (page 37): "Mr. Washington is hard-hearted and versatile. He assumed the appearance of lenity and forbearance—He had the power to crush all rivals and his jealousy made him employ it . . . . . The American buzzard must be stripped of his plumage . . . . . . Whether he continue a land jobber in Virginia

If the conjecture has any foundation that this pamphlet, either directly or indirectly, emanated from Arnold, then it is an impressive truth that, while no contemporary of Mr. Reed, those who died with him, or those who long survived him, ever was willing to countenance or repeat this gross charge, his last, as his first open accuser was He, who has the ineffable infamy of being the one American traitor, to whom every evil impulse and habit of our nature seems to have been traced, and in favour of whom not even a literary paradox has ever been suggested. There are no 'Historic Doubts' about Mr. Reed's worst apparent enemy, Benedict Arnold.

I am wrong in speaking of Arnold, as Mr. Reed's last accuser, for, on this point, Mr. George Bancroft, at the end of more than half a century, has taken up the thread of calumny—He finds it in the dark archives of Hesse Cassel.

Mr. Bancroft ostentatiously adduces, as proof of Mr. Reed's infidelity, a mutilated extract from what, he describes, as a 'Diary' of Count Donop, the Hessian commander of the advanced posts in New Jersey in December, 1776. He prints it, in the original, in a note to page 229 of his Ninth Volume. He gives no translation (as I shall) possibly because he was conscious that, in plain

or the President of Congress is to me indifferent." At page 53 he speaks of "the active enterprising Arnold, and the Frenchified Washington." My impression is that the pamphlet was written by some fugitive of the Charles Lee school, or, which is probable, though printed abroad, written in Philadelphia, where the chief disciples lived.

English, it amounted to nothing at all. There is always an ominous mystery in a foreign language which Mr. Bancroft does not hesitate to avail himself of.

Before I notice this subject in detail, let me allude to the view taken of such 'historical' evidence, by one Mr. Bancroft will hardly venture to discredit, and whom, rather ostentatiously, in his Preface he describes as his "friend" the late Jared Sparks. I have some doubts as to the extent of this friendship, but let that pass.

In 1864, Mr. Sparks, always alive to such matters, wrote to me:

"I am told that Mr. Bancroft has procured a copy of Donop's Journal. I should put no confidence in Donop's impressions or inferences unless sustained by the positive testimony of some written communication from General Reed. This is not likely to be produced. Donop might imagine motives which had no foundation in reality."

I will now show that even Donop did not imagine anything of the kind.

Mr. Bancroft thus introduces the Diary, which is to prove so much: "Diary kept in Donop's command, written by himself *or* one of his aids. The narration is very minute and exact," (page 217) Again he says, (page 229) "The Donop Diary, which is remarkably precise, full and accurate, alludes to Colonel Reed as having actually obtained a protection. This statement though made incidentally is positive and unqualified." Then follows the Hessian extract.

The reader will be surprised to learn, and to see, for I shall quote the very words in English, and Mr. Bancroft will not impugn the accuracy of the translation, that Count Donop, admitting the Diary to be his, made no such statement; but in fact alludes to the story as gossip at his Head-Quarters which he did not 'listen to,' and records it in connection with other matters which, we know, are utterly without foundation in truth.

I cite every word in the Donop Diary relating, directly or indirectly, to Mr. Reed.* There are four entries of the kind.

On the 20th December, the Diary says:

"December 20th.—Colonel Von Donop to day received by a flag of truce from the Rebel Colonel Reed, Adjutant General of Washington, a letter in which he, by authority of General Washington, proposed to have on the following day an interview with Colonel Donop on account of Burlington, as this place in the present situation was much exposed to both sides. It was left to Colonel Donop to determine time and place for such an interview. He answered immediately that his present situation did not permit him to leave his post. At the same time the letter of Colonel Reed was communicated, in which he proposed an interview about Burlington, and the answer given thereto; it was not to be presumed that the Rebels would try to hold Mount Holly and declare Burlington a neutral place, because from the small island near Bristol they could bombard Burlington with six pounders, while Mount Holly could be taken any time, if it was our pleasure to do so."

* It is due to Mr. Bancroft to say that, at my request made after the appearance of the 9th Volume, he sent me his Donop Note Book. I am thus enabled to give further extracts.

"December 25th.—To day a flag of truce was sent by Colonel Donop to Burlington offering to Colonel Reed the interview asked for as to that town, but an answer from Colonel Cadwalader that Reed was not there and was not expected to return before the next morning, he therefore would ask him to appoint another time and place for the interview."

All this is the record of what actually did take place, with the addition that it was done "by the authority of General Washington." I now come to the intermediate entry which I give, *verbatim*, and in English, and which Mr. Bancroft has the assurance to say is "precise," "full," "accurate," "positive" and "unqualified."

"December 21st.—Colonel Donop reported to General Grant that, notwithstanding it had been his intention to attack ('pay a visit to') General Putnam, he had desisted from such an enterprise after meeting Colonel Blork and Lieutenant Colonel Sterling at Mount Holly, and had received trustworthy information that the enemy had no more magazines this side the Delaware. It would not therefore be worth while to fatigue the troops who were already worn out and ragged. Moreover, it would be impossible for the troops to reach Cooper's Creek otherwise than by a circuitous route and muddy roads, for the bridges had all been destroyed. As his line was already extended from Bordentown to Black Horse, fourteen miles, he did not think it advisable to extend it further, and the less so because Rhall's Brigade was almost daily alarmed on both flanks."

So far what he says is pretty near the truth. Now for the camp gossip which Donop was unwilling to listen to, and I beg the reader to observe that the portion in *italics*, which shows that it was discredited hearsay, is carefully suppressed by Mr. Bancroft.

"*The reports about the enemy were so confused that he would not listen any more to them. Nevertheless, he would report that it was reported to him that during his stay at Mount Holly on the* 19*th inst.* 1000 *men, via Haddonfield and* 700 *via Moorestown, had been marching against Mount Holly for the purpose of attacking the two battalions at the Black Horse,* (*that*) *General Mifflin had advanced with one corps on the route leading to Moorestown to the bridge three miles from Mount Holly, but had done nothing except to destroy the bridge entirely;* (*that*) the Colonel Reed having received a protection, had come to meet General Mifflin and had declared that he did not intend any longer to serve; whereupon Mifflin is said to have treated him very harshly and even to have called him a damned rascal."

It is not surprising that Mr. Bancroft shrank from putting this trash in English, for it is very certain, and he knows it well, that it is a perfect cluster of false reports. On the 19th, 20th and 21st December, no force had advanced or was advancing *via* Haddonfield or from any other direction. Neither Mifflin, nor Putnam, nor any one had crossed the river, nor ever did cross the river till this chapter of adventure was closed. Count Donop treated these stories as idle tales which, while he or his aid noted, he did not listen to or believe. And yet, the American 'Historian of the Revolution,' picks out the one vague slander on his own countryman, and prints it as truth, suppressing the context which describes it as mere rumour, and a discredited rumour too! It would be a departure from the tone which should characterise historical discussion were I to describe in fitting terms my sense of this literary enormity.*

---

* There were other rumours floating around Donop's quarters and recorded in his Diary, which Mr. Bancroft does not reproduce. For

Without prolonging this unpleasant criticism, it should be noticed that General Mifflin, who is clumsily dragged into this scandal by the purveyors of false intelligence, was never called as a witness in 1782-3, that he lived long after, and with all his defects of charac-

example, in his Ninth Volume page 240, he says: "That day the term of enlistment of the Eastern regiments came to an end; to these veterans, the same conditions as Pennsylvania allowed to her undisciplined volunteers were offered if they would remain six weeks longer; and, with one voice, they instantly gave their word to do so, making no stipulation of their own." The Diary says: "December 24. Likewise also the New England men, or so called Yankees, have declared their determination on January 1, when their enlistment is at end, to go home. They have resolved to serve no more outside the limits of their own country." Now, which tells the truth, the History or the Diary? Is it only when a Southern man, for a Pennsylvanian was so regarded then, is to be maligned, that Mr. Bancroft quotes Hessian slander? True to his origin, he is reserved as to New England. There is another suppressed passage in the 'Donop Diary' which is material as showing further how little value there is in second-hand Hessian gossip. On the 28th of December, Donop reports to General Grant: "He has cause to regret that Colonel Sterling should be taken away from him, inasmuch as he shall thus lose not only a trusty friend, but also an interpreter of the English orders, as he himself is not sufficiently versed in that language, and had mainly to guess at the contents of the orders he received from General Grant, *and, as regards the news which from time to time was brought in by the inhabitants, he had the same difficulty*."

The 'diary' shows Donop to have been an active and vigilant officer, who thought it his duty to jot down and communicate all he heard, credible or incredible. Were I disposed to make minute criticisms, I might express a doubt whether, after all, the Colonel Reed of the Diary of the 21st December, was my ancestor, for according to Mr. Bancroft there were other Colonel Reeds. There was (page 246) 'the New England Reed.'

ter, and Revolutionary history shows they were many, he never condescended to fling calumny on the dead.*

In dismissing this subject, I beg the reader to observe that I have not condescended to dwell on the astounding fact, that, an American writer, who, on one page, records the brutality of these alien mercenaries, ('plundering ever since they landed in the country') for so, Mr. Bancroft describes the Germans, officers and men; on another, should ostentatiously cite a Hessian Colonel, or a Hessian Colonel's clerk, as a witness against his own countryman. The Hessian himself, as we have seen, did not believe the calumny which has been

* Mifflin died in 1800. My father, son of General Reed, was his friend, and the executor of his will. On the trial of Josiah Bright before Judge Washington in 1809, as reported by Lloyd, Mr. Ingersoll, the elder, in his speech for the defendant said: " In the Ninth Volume of the Journal of Congress, page 267, I observe that six States were against the claim of jurisdiction on the part of the Court of Appeal of Congress, and I find the name of Jefferson on the side of the question, for which I have the honour to contend; I add, last but not least, the names of Reed and Bryan. The patriot heart will joy at recollecting them; the former a wonderfully quick penetrating genius; the latter probably with the greatest fund of information of any man in the United States. I trust it will not detract from the weight of Mr. Reed's professional character that he was a soldier also in the war of the Revolution, and that the splendid military manœuvre adopted by Washington at Trenton, by which the fruits of a former victory were secured, and a second attained at Princeton, was of his suggestion. This information I received from General Mifflin who was himself a member of the council of war." My professional brethern know well who Mr. Ingersoll was—one of the leaders of the Ancient Bar—he was President Reed's intimate and valued friend. Surely his testimony is at least as trustworthy as Mr. Bancroft's Hessian hearsay.

raked up from the refuse of his camp. I hesitate, in conclusion, to ask the question and yet it is an obvious one—Does any one for a moment imagine that, had an officer of Mr. Reed's rank (Washington's Adjutant General) taken a protection or asked for one, or done anything of the kind, it would have remained a secret to this day? A protection was never granted without an antecedent oath, which was always matter of record.

Having thus, with what success it is not for me to say, disposed of the detailed evidence by which these calumnies have been propped up, I proudly turn to that, which after all is most conclusive—the well attested record of Mr. Reed's active life, on which has been thrown (a severe test for any public man) the strong, clear light of his domestic correspondence; the letters to and from his wife, and brothers, and kinsmen, and personal friends, for, in the biography which I published, I withheld no letter, however confidential and familiar, from any other reason than to avoid prolixity, or a fear of giving pain to the living by the revival of transient words or thoughts of asperity. That record is the best proof of my ancestor's public and private virtue—his patriotism in the highest and purest sense.

And to no part of the story of his Revolutionary service, do I more confidently refer than to that which tells what he, and those near and dear to him, did and suffered in those days of especial disaster, trial and victory, when it now seems, if posthumous libellers are to be credited, detraction was busiest with his fame; I mean the interval from the fall of Fort Washington to the retreat of the enemy to New Brunswick—from November, 1776, to January, 1777. With a brief reference to this, made more interesting by one or two letters which have come into my possession since the publication of my book in 1847, I conclude this effort at vindication.

After the fall of Fort Washington and the retreat of the American army through Eastern New Jersey, it seemed probable, in view of the advanced season and difficulties of transportation, (and within my recollection the winter roads north of Trenton and Princeton were practically impassable) that the Raritan would be the extreme limit of the British advance, and that the country between it and the Delaware would be a sort of neutral or border territory. As late as the 3rd of December, the enemy had not crossed the Raritan. Mr. Reed had been previously despatched to the fugitive Legislature of New Jersey to show the necessity of reinforcements. 'The critical situation of our affairs' wrote Washington to Governor Livingston, on the 23d of November, 1776 'and the movements of the enemy make some further and immediate exertions absolutely necessary. In order that you may have the fullest representation and form a perfect idea of what is now necessary, I have desired Colonel

Reed to wait on you and must refer you to him for particulars.' This duty, he had faithfully performed, and from Burlington, where his family then was and where Governor Livingston and his Assembly had been in session, Mr. Reed wrote his letter to Congress of the 28th of November, 1776, resigning his office of Adjutant General.* It is in these words:

To the President of Congress.

Burlington, New Jersey, November 28, 1776.

Sir,

Near three months ago, I laid before the committee of the honourable Congress, appointed to form and regulate the new army, my intentions of relinquishing the office of Adjutant General at the close of the campaign. The reasons then assigned, and which I should intrude upon your time to repeat, appeared to me so weighty that I conceived it a duty to the public and myself to represent them in the earliest and fullest manner.

As the season will not admit of further military operations (unless the enemy should attempt an incursion into this province to harass and distress us, in which case I shall most cheerfully devote myself to any further service) I beg leave to enclose the commission with the highest sense and warmest acknowledgments of the favour done me.

I am Sir, your most obedient and very humble servant,

Jos. Reed.

This letter, though dated on the 28th probably was not sent till the 30th. It had scarcely gone when a message was received from the Commander-in-Chief, that "invited by the broken state of our troops, the enemy had changed

---

* Governor Livingston's Letter, 27th Nov. 1776. Force, p. 870.

their plan and were rapidly advancing on the Delaware." On the first of December, Washington wrote to this effect to Governor Livingston, and it was probably by the bearer of that letter the message was sent to the Adjutant General. Mr. Reed did not hesitate, but instantly wrote—and it arrived in season—the following to Congress:

To the President of Congress.

Burlington, New Jersey, December 2, 1776.

Sir,

When I did myself the honour of addressing you on the 30th ult., I had not the least idea that the enemy would at this season attempt a progress thro' the country. It seems but too probable that I was mistaken. I therefore beg leave to retract the resignation I then made, and, as soon as I have disposed of Mrs. Reed and my children, will attend my office in the army until a successor is appointed or operations shall cease beyond all doubt.

Flattering myself that an uninterrupted attention for six months and my conduct during that time will incline you to the most favourable construction of this measure which proceeded from our unacquaintance of the state of things,

I am with great respect,

Your most obedient and very humble servant.

Jos. Reed.*

---

* Commenting on this, Mr. Bancroft says with more than ordinary venom: "(Reed) shrunk from his duty and seeking definitively to quit the army, sent back his commission to the President of Congress. But the prospect of unsparing censure, and a cold rebuke from Washington, who had seen proof of his disingenuousness, drove him, at the end of four days, to retract his resignation," p. 198. From all the evidence accessible to me and the statement of General Reed himself, I affirm this statement of a 'rebuke' from Washington, to be utterly groundless. If Mr.

The resignation of course was not accepted. The intentions of the enemy were rapidly developed, and on the 8th of December, Mr. Reed, having returned to Headquarters, wrote to the President of Congress:

Sir,

We set out this morning for Princeton. In our way we met a messenger with the enclosed. The General ordered me back upon some necessary business. He has gone forward to Princeton where there are about three thousand men with which I fear we will not be able to make a stand. The Jersey militia are so few that no dependence can be placed on them. The militia of Pennsylvania, except from the city, have not appeared and they are very confused, the time not having admitted of any arrangement. In short, sir, from all circumstances I am inclined to think no opposition will be given 'till we cross the Delaware. Our whole force if collected will not exceed six thousand, and they are diminishing every moment by desertion.

I can get no other paper than this—you will please to excuse it as well as the hurry of my letter.

I am, with much respect and regard, your most obedient humble servant. Jos. Reed.

Bancroft has any written or oral testimony as to it, let him produce it. If he has not, then his rhetorical assumption of such a fact, it seems to me, comes very close to the edge of wanton misrepresentation. The message which Mr. Reed describes had no rebuke in it, hot or cold. Washington's letter of the 30th does not allude to the subject. Slow to believe that Mr. Bancroft would invent this 'cold rebuke,' but, at the same time, confident that no such thing existed, I wrote an enquiry to my friend, the venerable Peter Force of Washington, whose answer is this: 'In reply to your questions in regard to the resignation of General Reed, in 1776, I might have answered it off hand, but I preferred to take time and make an examination. Beside the letters you referred to, I have found no letter or memorandum of General Washington, or any one else, on the subject of General Reed's resignation, in December, 1776. *Ms. letter*, 31 *December*, 1866.

Mr. Reed was then sent to Philadelphia to urge activity in reinforcements, and with the news of the retreat of the Americans to the right bank of the Delaware. From that time, 'till the 12th, he was either with the Commander-in-Chief, or on such detached special duty as their confidential relations and Mr. Reed's thorough acquaintance with the neighbouring region imposed on him. It must have been during one of these expeditions that he wrote to Washington the following hurried letter, which I had not seen in 1847, but which I find in Mr. Force's Archives; my impression is that it was written at either Newtown or some point above Trenton.

REED TO WASHINGTON.

December, 12, 1776.

DEAR SIR,

The gentlemen of the Light Horse who went into the Jerseys have returned safe. They proceeded into the country 'till they met an intelligent person directly from Trenton, who informed them that General Howe was then with the main body of his army; that the flying army, consisting of the Light Infantry and grenadiers, under Lord Cornwallis, still lay at Pennytown and there was no appearance of a movement. That they are certainly waiting for boats from Brunswick; that he believed they would attempt a landing in more places than one; that their artillery park has thirty pieces of cannon—all field pieces. They are collecting horses from all parts of the country. Some movement was intended yesterday morning but laid aside; but what it was and why they did not proceed he does not know. I sent off a person to Trenton yesterday morning with directions to return by Pennytown. I told him to go to . . . . . . and get what intelligence he could from him. He is not yet returned. I expect him every moment. I charged him to let . . . . . . know that, if he would watch their motions and could inform us of the time and place of their proposed landing, he should receive a large reward for which I would be answerable. I cannot but think their landing will be between this and Trenton, for these reasons:

1st. That Lord Cornwallis with that part of the army which he will lead, keeps at Pennytown, within four miles of the river.

2nd. They will by that means avoid the ferry at Shamony, and the fords which, at this season of the year, must be disagreeable to the troops.

3rd. They will derive much more assistance from the country which is but too favourable to them.

4th. They know our principal artillery is near Trenton and the passage through the woods to Bristol must be unfavourable to them. On the road above they will find all clear and the distance nearly the same.

The river is not and I believe cannot be sufficiently guarded. We must depend upon intelligence of their motions; to obtain which no expense must be spared. If it were possible to fix signals answering to their different movements, that would be most speedy and effectual. The militia are crossing over in parties. I fear they do not mean to return. I do not know by whose orders, but if their Colonels have power to give permission, in a little time there will be none left. I do not like the condition of things at and above Coryell's Ferry; the officers are quite new and seem to have little sense of the necessity of vigilance. I shall wait a little to see my man return, and then, unless your Excellency think my stay here of service, I will return to Headquarters. I enclose you a proclamation which I got from the other side. I suppose it is one of the same kind General Dickerson saw. Mr. Moylan desires me to mention to your Excellency the propriety of his meeting General Lee to inform him of the state of things, and wishes to know your plan by the return of the Light Horse.

I am in haste, most respectfully, Dear Sir,

Your obedient, humble, servant,

Jos. Reed.

On the 14th, news was received of Lee's capture, and, some time in that week, Mr. Reed was sent to Bristol to assist and counsel with General Cadwalader, whose command consisted mainly of Pennsylvania, indeed Philadelphia militia—his and Mr. Reed's townsmen and neighbours. This is a simple and natural explanation of the arrangement. The distance from Head-Quarters was very short, nine miles when at Newtown, and ten if opposite Trenton; if Doctor Rush is to be credited, the Adjutant General being in constant connection with the Commander-in-Chief. That General Cadwalader, writing in 1783, hinted a sinister object in Mr. Reed's joining him, is very true, but it is one of the worst specimens of unproved insinuation with which his pamphlet abounds. Mr. Reed did assist him actively and faithfully, and I have little doubt, from the evidence accessible to me, that the high spirited soldier of 1776, for such was General John Cadwalader, never harboured the thought or suspicion, or to his nearest friend whispered the insinuation which fell from the tongue of the angered partisan of 1778 and '83. While at Bristol, on the 22d of December, Mr. Reed wrote to Washington what I may describe as the 'Pomroy' letter, (*supra*, page 43,) to which and to what I have said of it, I specially refer the reader. It's first effect was that Reed was sent for to Head-Quarters and the outlines of the plan of attack on Trenton communicated to him, and at the same time, it is said, a letter was written to the same purport to Cadwalader. Then followed, with General Cadwalader's full concurrence, the night visit of Mr. Reed and Colonel Cox to Griffin at Mount Holly—and then, probably on their return to camp at Bristol, came Washington's remarkable letter of anxious inquiry and affectionate confidence, addressed to "Joseph Reed, Esq.—or in his absence, John Cadwalader, Esq., only"—in its fading but still clear characters, now before me, and which, tho' often printed before, I cannot resist the temptation to reproduce. It was to these two friends only—friends of his, and as he thought, of each other—that he told the perilous secret of his necessities and his intentions, and of the very hour, almost the minute, he meant to execute his plan of adventure.

Camp above Trenton Falls, 23d December,1776.

DEAR SIR,

The bearer is sent down to know whether your plan was attempted last night, and if not, to inform you that Christmas day, at night, one hour before day, is the time fixed upon for our attempt on Trenton. For heaven's sake keep this to yourself, as the discovery of it may prove fatal to us. Our numbers, sorry I am to say, being less than I had any conception of; but necessity, dire necessity, will—nay must justify any attempt. Prepare and in concert with Griffin attack as many of their posts as you possibly can, with a prospect of success. The more we attack at the same instant, the more confusion we shall spread, and the greater good will result from it.

If I had not been fully convinced before of the enemy's designs, I have now ample testimony of their intentions to attack Philadelphia as soon as the ice will afford the means of conveyance.

As the Colonels of the Continental regiments might kick up some dust about command, unless Cadwalader is considered by them in the light of a Brigadier, which I wish him to be, I desired General Gates, who is unwell and applied for leave to go to Philadelphia, to endeavour, if his health would permit him, to call and stay two or three days at Bristol in his way.

I shall not be particular. We could not ripen matters for our attack before the time mentioned in the first part of this letter. So much out of sorts, and so much in want of everything are the troops under Sullivan, &c. Let me know by a careful express the plan you are to pursue. The letter herewith sent, forward on to Philadelphia. I could wish it to be in, in time for the Southern post's departure, which will be, I believe, by eleven o'clock to morrow.

    I am, dear sir,
      Your most obedient servant,
        GEO. WASHINGTON.

P. S. I have ordered our men to be provided with three days provisions, ready cook'd; with which and their blankets, they are to march; for if we are successful, which Heaven grant, and other circumstances favour, we may push on. I shall direct every ferry and ford to be well guarded, and not a soul suffered to pass without an officer going down with the permit. Do the same with you.

To JOSEPH REED, ESQ.,
  or, in his absence, to
    JOHN CADWALADER, ESQ., only, at Bristol.*

---

* I am unable to estimate the logic by which it is assumed that this letter was so addressed because Washington thought Cadwalader might be

When this letter came, it was known at Bristol that Griffin had retired and that there was no hope of concert from him. It was then determined that, while Cadwalader matured a movement in aid of Washington in the neighbourhood of Burlington, Reed should go to Philadelphia and persuade Putnam, who was in command, to cross at Cooper's Ferry. This was on the night of the 24th, and from Philadelphia, Mr. Reed wrote to Cadwalader the next morning:

"General Putnam has determined to cross the river with as many men as he can collect, which he says will be about five hundred; he is now mustering and endeavouring to get Proctor's company of artillery to go with them. I wait to know what success he meets with and the progress he makes—but at all events I shall be with you this afternoon."*

absent. It would then have been to 'John Cadwalader, Esq., or in his absence to Joseph Reed, Esq.,' and in the text 'Cadwalader' would not have been spoken of in the third person. It is not at all material. I am tempted to add a brief extract from Washington's earnest letter to Congress, the next day, to show what troops he relied on, in this the hour of agony, if not despair. "By the departure of these regiments (Lee's and Gates's corps) I shall be left with five from *Virginia*, Smallwood's from *Maryland*, a small part of Rawlins' and Hand's from *Pennsylvania*, part of *Ward's* from *Connecticut*, and the German battalion, amounting in the whole at this time to from 1400 to 1500 effective men. This handful and such militia as may choose to join me, will then compose our army." I find no allusion to the 'Mariners from Marblehead.' Mr. Bancroft quotes the language of Washington's letter of the 23d, but takes pains to avoid saying it was addressed to Reed.

* The rest of this letter has never been printed. The extract I find in the Cadwalader pamphlet.

This was but doubtful encouragement—Five hundred men, with or without artillery, was all that could be expected, and their movements were uncertain.—Well might Mr. Reed say what he did, years afterwards in his pamphlet (page 18,) and well might he send, for it was his duty to tell the exact truth, 'discouraging accounts' to Washington, though, from the date of the letter from McKonkey's Ferry (25th, 6 P. M.,) it is probable the news there referred to, related to Griffin's withdrawal, and not to Putnam's delay. "At all events," wrote Mr. Reed, "I shall be with you this afternoon," and he kept his word, and was at Bristol and the Ferry taking part in the ice-blocked passage of that winter night, the incidents of which and of the adventurous advance to Burlington, have already been described. Whilst the troops below were ineffectually struggling with the elements, Washington had crossed above and by noon of the next day (26th) had consummated his victory at Trenton. The sound of the firing was heard, but the news of the precise result did not reach Bristol whither Mr. Reed had returned, 'till some time on the 27th, or at night of the 26th. The rest of the narrative of those days has been elsewhere given, and as the object of what I now write is merely defensive, I shall not repeat it, the end being the pursuit of the enemy almost to the banks of the Hudson; in every step and movement of which Mr. Reed shared with Cadwalader, under the eye of Washington.

Accident has thrown in my way the following letters, which have never been published, and which are not without interest.

They need but a word of explanatory comment.

It will be recollected that, in Mr. Reed's pamphlet of 1782, in reference to his visit to Philadelphia, at midnight of the 24th of December, this passage occurs:

"I lay down for a few hours, and when the morning came, a number of gentlemen, among whom I particularly recollect Colonel Moylan, Mr. James Mease and Mr. R. Peters, came, and anxiously enquired into our situation and prospects. They can tell whether despondency or animation, hope or apprehension, most prevailed, and whether the language I held was not the very reverse of despair; the former may remember, that when urged to stay and partake of a social entertainment provided for the day, I declared my resolution that no consideration should prevent my return to the army immediately; and that in a private conversation I pressed him to do the same, lest he should lose a glorious opportunity to serve his country and distinguish himself. I was not at liberty to be perfectly explicit, but the hint was sufficient to a brave officer."

This 'brave officer'—Stephen Moylan of Pennsylvania, was one of Mr. Reed's life-long friends. The recollections of this friendship, and the allusion in the passage I have just cited, tempt me to print the following very characteristic letter.

Colonel Moylan to Robert Morris.

Headquarters, Morristown, January 7, 1777.

Dear Sir,

I thank you, my good friend, for your favour of the first. What a change in our affairs, since the date of that letter. Are you not all too happy? By Heavens, it was the best piece of generalship I ever read or heard of. An enemy, within musket shot of us, determined, and only waiting for daylight, to make a vigourous attack. We stole a march, got to Princeton, defeated, and almost totally ruined, three of the best regiments in the British service; made all their schemes upon Philadelphia, for this season, abortive; put them into such a consternation, that if we only had five hundred fresh men, there is very little doubt but we should have destroyed all their stores and baggage, at Brunswick, of course, oblige them to leave the Jerseys, (this they must do) and probably have taken poor Naso.* What would our worthy General have given for 500 of the fellows who were eating beef and pudding at Philadelphia on that day? But let us not repine—it was glorious. The consequence must be great. America will—by G—d—it must be free!

I never mentioned my desire to the General of engaging in the cavalry. Your letter, I believe, gave him the first intimation. I put it into his hands to show him your gift of divination. Pray, how could you suppose, that our next blow must be at Princeton, but I recollect you did not then know we were attacked at Trenton. How your heart went pitipat, when that news reached you, and what an agreeable feeling you must all have had when you heard of their facing right about. But that feeling is very short of those which we all enjoyed when pursuing the flying enemy. It is unutterable—inexpressible. I know I never felt so much like one of Homer's deities before. We trod on air—it was a glorious day. Pray send us back those runaways that left us these some days past. We are really weak, strengthen our hands, and we will not leave an enemy out of gunshot from their ships. I will not tire you further than telling you what I have often done, that

I am sincerely, Sir, yours,

To Robert Morris, Esq.   STEPHEN MOYLAN.

* Charles Lee.

Mr. Bancroft of course has a fling at Colonel Moylan. The reader cannot fail to be struck with the number and virulence of his minute defamations. It is a sort of eruptive disease with him. He assails, besides Mr. Reed *passim*, Greene pp. 40, 174, 184-5, 8, 9, 193-4, 5, 426-8, Dickinson pp. 46, 199, Mercer p. 113, Smallwood p. 123, Lambert Cadwalader p. 190, St. Clair p. 246, Mifflin pp. 39, 459, Armstrong p. 106, Sullivan p. 397. Moylan and Wayne p. 230, 456, every one, except Greene from Rhode Island and Sullivan from New Hampshire, born south of the Hudson. Wayne's offence to Mr. Bancroft may be his letter to Gates of the first of December, 1776, printed in Mr. Force's Archives. "Whilst I am writing, an express brings advice of Fort Washington being in the hands of the enemy, and the whole garrison consisting of 2000 men killed or prisoners. My heart bleeds for poor Washington. Had he but Southern troops, he would not be necessitated so often to fly before an enemy who, I fear, has lately had but too much reason to hold us cheap." Bancroft, speaking of General Ewing, says: "He did not even make an attempt to cross at Trenton." Washington, writing to Congress, says: "The quantity of ice was so great that, though General Ewing did every thing in his power to effect it, he could not get over."*

A fortnight later, Mr. Reed, then probably acting as

---

* Works of Washington, Vol. 4, page 247.

Adjutant General till his successor was named—and at all events at Headquarters, wrote the following semi-official letter to Philadelphia, which has this interest, that it shows how kindly, how generously, and I am quite willing to say, how justly he thought and wrote of his fellow-soldiers, of some of those who became so soon his bitter enemies.

To Mr. Thomas Bradford, Printer.
"Sir,

I am directed by his excellency, General Washington, to forward to you the enclosed, with a request that they may be printed in the public papers, with a note that all printers of newspapers will re-print them in their several papers—and that you would have 1000 copies of each struck off and forwarded to him with all possible expedition. The evils they are calculated to remedy are of so alarming and increasing a nature that no time is to be lost.

I shall be much obliged to you to remind your father that there are two new blankets among his baggage belonging to me. I shall be obliged to him to secure them for me if they are to be found.

We have nothing new in this quarter, our parties every day harrass the enemy; yesterday one of them attacked 600 of the enemy near Woodbridge, after a warm firing our troops retreated, the enemy's number being three times superior. The stormy weather will, I fear, give the remainder of the Philadelphia militia a very bad march home. The last moved off yesterday, having greatly distinguished themselves by their gallant behaviour in the field, as well as orderly and soldierlike conduct in camp. All the militia are following their example in annoying the enemy every opportunity, so that we hope in a little time they will prove a noble support to their country. General Cadwalader has conducted his command with great honour to himself and the Province, all the field officers supported their characters, their example was followed by the inferior officers and men, so that they have returned with the thanks and praises of every general officer in the army.

The Light Horse, tho' few in number, have rendered as essential service, as in my opinion, the same number of men ever performed to their country in the same time. They thought no duty beneath them, and went through it with a generous disregard of fatigue and danger, which entitles them to the kindest notice and attention of their fellow citizens. We hope that some of the artillery officers who have engaged in this temporary service may be induced to enter into the Continental army as the specimen they have given shows that they may be exceedingly useful to their country in a line of service which every day shows to be more and more important.

It might appear invidious to mention names where all have behaved well—but Colonel Morgan, Colonel Nixon, Colonel Cox, your old gentleman,* and Major Knox, and Cowperthwaite, certainly ought not to pass unnoticed for their behaviour at Princeton. Major Meredith would, on many accounts, be a great acquisition to the army if he could be prevailed on to engage in the service, he has a military turn and, tho' he was diffident of himself, it appeared when we came to action that there was not the least foundation for it, but quite the reverse.

I am Sir, with esteem,
Your most obedient, humble servant,
JOS. REED.

Headquarters, Morristown, January 24, 1777.

The next month, after more than a year's dispersal, Mr. Reed and his family found themselves for a time at home in Philadelphia. There are now before me two manuscripts, for which I am indebted to a kinswoman (alas! now dead) in a distant land, letters

* The William Bradford who made the affidavit of 1782. Ante. p. 28.

from the husband and father, the wife and mother of that re-united family, which came into my possession more than seventy years after those who wrote them sank into their graves, and which I now reprint as homely testimonials of fidelity and heroism. They are both written to Mrs. Reed's brother, Mr. De Berdt of London; for in those times, unlike ours, the refined cruelty of prohibiting correspondence of relatives on different sides of Civil War was not resorted to.*

Mr. Reed to Mr. De Berdt.

Philadelphia, February 20, 1777.

Dear Dennis,

It is not one of the least misfortunes of these unhappy times in which our lot is cast, that the intercourse of the nearest relations and dearest friends is almost wholly interrupted. Except your letter by Lord Howe, and your packet by Israel Morris, we have heard nothing from you for almost twelve months. However it is no small consolation to us to learn that your prospects of business are exceeding good while ours are changed from the most prosperous to the most adverse. The war being brought to our own door, and carried on with the most inhuman ravage, in which age and sex have indiscriminately suffered, has banished every idea of law, so that the profession for which it has been my earliest study to qualify myself is become entirely useless. The family, as well for safety as economy, have been obliged to leave Philadelphia, but, unluckily directing its course into the Jerseys, which, soon after, the British and Hessian Troops penetrated; your mother—sister—five children, were again obliged to fly, and are now secluded from all society but among themselves, surrounded with woods and inhabitants of the common

---

* I recovered these letters through the kind offices of the granddaughter of Mr. de Berdt, Mrs. Esther Reed Merriman—Mrs. Merriman died near London, in 1862.

class of country people. I thank God they have experienced little distress but what arises from fatigue or apprehension. A party of the Hessian Troops came into the town of Burlington the next day after they left, and afterwards were within three miles of their retreat. To have been plundered of everything they could carry away, and the destruction of what they could not, was the least in such case to be expected—but happily the American arms at this crisis proved successful; the enemy was obliged to evacuate this country, and peace and quiet have been restored, but how long it will last none can tell but He who knows all things. Your letter by Lord Howe arrived before there had been any effusion of blood; it was wrote with a spirit and sentiment that would do you honour among the sensible and dispassionate. I was then with the army, and after showing it to the General, I transmitted it to the Congress, but no notice was taken of it. I then waited impatiently for a public disclosure of some terms or propositions from Lord Howe and his brother. If they had been such as would give my country any security against the unlimited powers of your Parliament to deprive us of our property at any time and in what proportions they pleased, I should have applied myself most earnestly to have brought about an accommodation, and if those in power had wantonly or wickedly rejected the proposition, I should have retired from the army to a private and obscure station. But no such proposition being ever made, tho' general professions of kindness and justice were profusely given, and being well satisfied in my own mind, from a conversation I had with the Adjutant General of the British Army, whom I conducted to and from an interview with General Washington, that the commissioners had no powers to give liberty, peace and safety to this country, I no longer hesitated about my duty, but continued with the army the whole campaign, and have been in every action except two which has happened during the whole summer. I thank God I have enjoyed uninterrupted health, and met with no accident. But the office I hold not being agreeable to me, and my doing what I deemed my duty, having made me many enemies among the intractable and undisciplined part of our army, I resolved to decline it when the campaign was over. In what line I shall hereafter move is very uncertain, but the dispute is now advanced to such a heighth, and the inhumanity with which it has been conducted by the British Generals has created such an inveteracy between the two countries as no (*illegible*) can efface. The British Nation must receive its impression from its officers and friends. They have injured us so highly by their ravages, cruelty and insult that it is impossible they can ever forgive us, for there is no hatred so deadly as that of him who has injured another, and is conscious he can neither palliate or redress it. The scenes of cruelty and desolation, which my own eyes have beheld, are beyond description. The havoc which avarice, lust and wantonness have made in this fine growing country, will be remembered for ages —if its progress should cease to morrow. The illiberal abuse of the King and his Ministers I detest—a false ambition and a mistaken idea of the true interest of the Nation has led them astray, but History shews us that this is no novelty. I fear national pride must also be taken into the account—that pride which being transplanted to this country shews our descent, and perhaps is not unjustly termed obstinacy. In this state of things where can the man of honour and lover of his country set his foot? On the one hand an unlimited submission which scarcely leaves a shadow of liberty—on the other a dreadful opposition subversive of every species of social and commercial happiness, and of which no end is yet to be seen—those who prefer temporary ease and safety to essential liberty would find no difficulty in the choice; but how can a man of honour, and who thinks himself bound to transmit to his posterity the blessings of freedom unimpaired make the ignominious sacrifice?

Adieu my Dear Dennis.

     Most affect'y Yours.

Mrs. Reed to Mr De Berdt.

"An opportunity of writing to you, my dear Dennis, is now become so rare, that I could not think of letting this slip without sitting down to tell you our distresses. How shall I describe our situation for some months past; your heart, I am sure, has already felt much for us, but you could not form any adequate idea of the scenes we have pass'd. Thank God our apprehensions and fears have not been altogether realized, but these were sufficient; but one day's escape from an army of foreigners, and, for several weeks, within a few hours march of them, and since they have been driven back, we have understood they had planned a visit to our retreat. Nothing could be more distressing but the dreadful reality; but a kind and overruling Providence protected us from the dangers we feared, and our retreat has been safe and comfortable; anything more we hardly dared to wish. Since the happy change in our affairs we look back without regret on our past distresses, and trust to the same Almighty Power which so evidently appeared then in our favour to deliver us from the hand of oppression which lately threatened to strike us to the dust. You will be surprised, I dare say, at the rapid and uninterupted progress the enemy made thro' this province, but when I tell you the horrid blunder our Rulers made, it will easily account for it; they enlisted their soldiers for a short time, some four, some six months; the enemy, as might readily be supposed, were informed of this, and at the time our army was disbanding and did not consist of more than 3000 men, they marched thro' and took possession of the Province—what has happened since, and the happy change in which our arms have proved successful, you will hear from many quarters. Our prospects are brighter, our hopes are raised, our utmost efforts are exerting, and we devoutly trust in the favour and assistance of the Great Arbiter and Ruler of Nations, who alone can give success to our arms and peace to our land.

Our domestic affairs have another change by the addition of a daughter, which happened just at the time my dear Mr. Reed was exposed to all the dangers and fatigues of a campaign. A kind Providence has preserved both our lives and we are now enjoying a few weeks together in peace and safety, but it is not without many anxious fears for the future. I cannot forget to tell you that Mr. Reed has had some very narrow escapes of his life, once by one of our own men who was running away and he ordered to return to his duty, the fellow presented his musket within half a yard of his head, but it happily missed fire, and another time in an engagement near N. Y. his horse was shot under him. But however great and complicated our difficulties and distresses have been, we have not been so fully taken up by them, but we have truly and affectionately shared in your happier prospects, and are anxious to hear that your hopes and expectations both in love and business are answered. Adieu, adieu, my dear Dennis, I know not when I shall have another opportunity of writing to you; you must embrace every one of writing to us—I need not tell you that our Dear Mama remembers you with the utmost tenderness, or that I am,

With the sincerest affection,
Ever Yours,
E. REED.

In less than a year after this, Mr. Reed's Administration as President of the Executive Council of Pennsylvania, began. It continued by unanimous re-election for three years, and to its record of untiring and successful public service, I again appeal.

One word more on two minor matters which the purveyors of slanderous gossip, including Mr. Bancroft, have made subject of incidental misrepresentation,—the allegations that Mr. Reed, when Adjutant General, stimulated local prejudices amongst the Continental troops, especially at the expense of the New England levies; and that there was an actual interruption of friendly relations between General Washington and him, in consequence of a discovery said to have been made as to the

Lee letter. This fiction is, I believe, due to the imagination of Mr. John C. Hamilton who, conscious that between his ancestor and Washington there had been a personal difference, in no sense creditable to the younger man, conjured up this notion of a quarrel with Mr. Reed.

The first imputation is to be found in a note to the Cadwalader pamphlet, and in a letter from Joseph Trumbull, an aid of Charles Lee, which has been recently and ostentatiously printed in the "resurrection" of 1863.* Both of these I refer to, with the passing comment that John Adams, who is quoted, was Doctor Rush's intimate friend, and that they were members of Congress when Mr. Reed was named as a Brigadier. The gossip is a curious confirmation of a remark somewhere made by Mr. Jay, in writing to Washington about Congress, that "there is as much intrigue as at the Vatican, and as much secrecy as in a boarding School."

The two charges, such as they are, shall be noticed in order.

I. As to the New England troops. It is better on

---

* This Joseph Trumbull seems to have been possessed with the spirit of sectionalism. "It is said" he wrote on 18 November, 1776, "that Mount Washington has surrendered. We don't yet learn particulars. I am glad a *Southern* officer commanded. The story is not told to his advantage here; be it as it may, we should not have heard the last of it from Reed and some others of his stamp, if a New England man had commanded." The two 'Southern' officers in command were Magaw and Lambert Cadwalader, both Pennsylvanians.

this as on other questions, to allow Mr. Reed to make his own defence. In a letter addressed to Congress on the subject of military promotion, in the spring or summer following the events I have endeavoured to describe, he used this language:

"While the camp was stationary and danger at a distance, some crimes could not exist and others could not be prevented or punished; but when the approach of the enemy brought in the militia without any tincture of discipline; when the hurry of retreat or action made it difficult to go thro' the forms of trial, all restraints seemed to be broken down. A spirit of desertion, cowardice, plunder and shrinking from duty when attended with fatigue or danger, prevailed but too generally thro' the whole army. And why should I disguise any part of the truth by concealing that it was more conspicuous in one part of the army than another? The Orderly Books and concurrent testimony of the impartial and sensible officers, even among themselves, will prove it. In this state of things when military justice was in a great degree suspended, and the discipline, the safety of the army, depended upon the private virtue and exertions of the officers, rather than the coercion of Government, it cannot be thought surprising that, in very populous States, many should have got into offices and commissions, who would prove unworthy of them in an hour of such severe trial, and endanger the service and distress this Command. Answerable as I was for the safety of this army, so far as it depended upon its guards—called by the duty of my office and orders, ten times repeated, to exert myself in preventing and punishing the great military offences I have noted before—I did speak freely, tho' generally in private, to such officers as failed in their duty by absence from camp on pretence of sickness, and brought to trial without favour, every officer or soldier who was charged with cowardice, fraud, plunder of the publick stores, or the poor inhabitants. There was not a person in this wide Continent more anxious than myself to extinguish all distinctions except those which merit and service create; but it is impossible—it is too deeply rooted ever to be eradicated. I thought it not amiss to avail myself of what could not be remedied, and endeavoured to draw emulation from that source. The ignorant, the timid and the lazy, convinced that I am not vulnerable should they attempt to enter into particulars, took occasion to charge me with creating disunion and division. Had my conversation embittered the mind of the General, or private correspondence those of any members of Congress—had it been the subject of open invidious comparison to officers of other Provinces, or even of private letters to my friends at home, there might be some colour for the charge, but my soul is above such practices; what I said was to the faulty or their friends, openly and above all disguise, proceeding from an honest tho' perhaps too zealous a hope of amendment on points, which if not amended, must, sooner or later, end in the destruction of the Army, and finally of the cause itself."*

It is surely not necessary at this time of day to justify, by evidence, language so clear and explicit. Washington's letters are full of it; candid New England historians admit the existence of a levelling and unmilitary spirit, and, if specific proof of the disorganization, to use a mild word, of some of the New England troops be needed, I turn to the testimony of Colonel Joseph Trumbull himself, the witness produced against Mr. Reed, who makes to his father, the Governor, this revelation:

Honoured Sir,

Enclosed I send you returns of some of the regiments of Connecticut Militia, under command of Major-General Wooster, such as I can get; though I have called and called, again and again, for them, I believe there is but one of them which is really true, that is Major Brinsmade's, who seems to be the honestest man. The fact is they cannot make their weekly and provision returns agree; for this reason, they have made a number of brevet officers. They doubt whether these officers will be allowed extra rations; to avoid this, they return so many more men as to cover the extra rations for these officers. You'll see by adverting to these returns that some companies have more officers than privates at best; but not content with that, and instead of sending home

---

* "It is impossible for any one to have an idea of the complete equality which exists between the officers and men who compose the greater part of our troops. You may form some notion of it when I tell you that yesterday morning a Captain of Horse, who attends the General, was seen shaving one of his own men near the house." *Letter to Mrs. Reed, October* 11, 1776.

the officers who have very few men, and turning those men over into other companies, they add brevet officers, not only to pick the pockets of the public here, but also, by and by, these brevet officers are to be dismissed from the militia rolls at home, and in a few times more being called forth, there will be no militia left in the State.*

On this head, I have no more to say.

II. The alienation from Washington. This is more plainly stated by Mr. John C. Hamilton than by any other writer, tho' Mr. Bancroft takes up the strain. Mr. Hamilton is the only one who enters into imaginary particulars—gives a reason for his assumed facts and fixes an exact date—the month of November, 1780; as to which, I merely observe that even a moderately anxious inquirer after historical truth will need, and has a right to require, better evidence to establish either facts, dates, or theories, than Mr. Hamilton's averments. No one knows this better than Mr. Bancroft. If, among the Hamilton papers or elsewhere, there is a written word confirmatory of this alienation and its imputed cause, the Lee correspondence, it can easily be produced. Till it is, I have a right to put it in the category of unscrupulous defamations. It is certainly true that after November 1780, the private correspondence of Washington and Reed, in a measure, ceased, but any one who will take the trouble,

---

* 4th December, 1776. Forces' Archives, 5th Series, Vol. page 3, 1073.

as I have had occasion to do, to examine the Archives of Pennsylvania while Mr. Reed was President, will see how constant and unreserved the public correspondence was, and I think it is clear from an inspection of Mr. Sparks' work, that towards the close of the War, Washington's private correspondence with his friends everywhere very much diminished. When, in August, 1780, President Reed marched to Trenton with the Pennsylvania Militia, his correspondence with his wife, printed in my Memoir, indicated a transient uneasiness as to some slight alienation on the part of General Washington.* With this exception, I do not find the least trace of the difference which the busy and malevolent men of this day have insinuated, and am aware of no cause for anything of the kind. General Sullivan, between whom and Mr. Reed, there appears not to have been a friendly feeling, had written accusatory letters to Washington in 1779, but they evidently made no impression, for there were in them allegations as to the Conway cabal, which Washington knew to be groundless.† Mr. Reed had nothing whatever to do, directly or indirectly, with the Conway cabal.

---

* Life of Reed, Vol. II., page 248. In 1781, writing to Greene, President Reed said: "Washington complains of us all." (Id. pp. 358.) Still later in the same year he writes: "The incessant mirepresentations and calumnies with respect to myself, and some unfriendly characters about him have raised prejudices, of what nature I cannot tell, but this does not hinder my revering his character and doing justice to his merits and services. May he long and happily enjoy the laurels he has acquired." (Id. page 373.)

† *Sparks'* "*Letters to Washington*," Vol. 2, page 366, 280.

His enemies, such as Doctor Rush, were deeply implicated in it. Late in November, 1780, at least after the 22d, Mrs. Washington was the guest of Mr. Reed.* In October, 1781, Mr. Reed wrote to felicitate Washington on his victory over Cornwallis, and received the following reply:

Mount Vernon, 15 November, 1781.

DEAR SIR,

    I have the honour to thank you most sincerely for your congratulations conveyed in your favour of the 27th ult. That our success against the enemy in the State of Virginia has been so happily effected, and with so little loss—and that it promises such favourable consequences, (if properly improved,) to the welfare and independence of the United States—is matter of very pleasing reflection. I beg you to be assured that I am, with perfect regard and esteem

    Dear Sir, your most obedient

        Humble servant,

TO HON. JOSEPH REED, ESQ.   GEO. WASHINGTON.†

---

* *Voyage de Chastellux*, Vol. I., 161.

† In writing a formal letter to the Executive Council, Washington said: "I most sincerely thank you for your kind wishes for my personal prosperity, and beg you to be assured that a full establishment of peace, liberty and independence, to this and the other United States of America, is my most ardent wish." In March, 1782, the following item is to be found in the Philadelphia newspapers: "Last Friday morning, His Excellency General Washington left this City, attended by the Honourable General Potter, Vice President of the State, General Reed, the late President, a number of gentlemen, officers of the Army, and also Captain Morris' Troop of City Light Horse." *Freeman's Journal*, 27 *March*, 1782. When Washington resigned his commission at Anapolis, he said: "While I repeat my obligations to the Army in general, I should do injustice to my own feelings not to acknowledge in this place the peculiar services and distinguished merits of the gentlemen

During the spring and summer of the next year, I am aware of no correspondence, Washington being, from time to time, in Philadelphia. In September, 1782, there were two letters with reference to this Cadwalader controversy, which may here with propriety be inserted, with no other comment than that they show, on one side, the consciousness of innocence which frankly and confidently appeals for justice, and on the other, the friendly readiness with which the appeal was met. It will be remembered that in General Cadwalader's reply to Mr. Reed, not a word of comment is made on Washington's letter.

Reed to Washington.

September 11, 1782.

Dear Sir,

After the services, sufferings, and anxieties of the winter of 1776, I little expected that period would be selected as the season of my greatest reproach, and that I should stand publicly charged with not only meditating, but actually expressing intentions of deserting to the enemy. Yet, sir, so it is; not mere newspaper abuse, or transient report, but actually countenanced and supported by a person of some rank and appearance in the world. Having never asked or received any public favour from Congress, conscious of my own integrity, and deeply wounded with the cruel suggestion, I must appeal to your justice and candour, and most earnestly request you would, by the bearer, who goes express for the purpose, favour me with a few lines expressive of your sense of my con-

who have been attached to my person during the War. It was impossible the choice of confidential officers to compose my family should have been more fortunate."

duct in the fall and winter of the year 1776; and particularly whether you ever heard, or at any time entertained doubts of my fidelity, and whether under the communications made to me of our military operations, an apprehended treachery on my part would not have made me a very dangerous character.

I would farther beg you would permit my making use of sundry letters I have received from you, at a time when you appeared to repose an unreserved confidence in me, and of which, I can appeal to that God who knows the secrets of all hearts, I was not (in point of integrity) unworthy.

As I never availed myself of your Excellency's friendship to seek for honour or profit, or even for the reparation of losses actually sustained in the service, I have the fullest confidence that you will most cheerfully comply with this, to me, most interesting request; and should you descend to particulars, you will be pleased to point them to the period which intervened between our retreat from Hackensack, and the revival of our affairs at Princeton.

My memory suggests to me a letter I wrote your Excellency from Bristol, containing reasons for an attack on the enemy; if that letter can be obtained, I am persuaded it contains sentiments of a very different nature from those of which I complain, and would be particularly useful.*

I shall make no other use of any communication I now have, or you may favour me with, than to vindicate my own character against the malignant imputation of intending a desertion to the enemy. And am,

With the greatest respect,

Your Excellency's humble servant,

JOSEPH REED.

---

* This was the "Pomroy" letter, the history of which I have already given—*supra page* 43.

Washington to Reed.

Verplanck's Point, 15 *September,* 1782.

Dear Sir,

The appeal contained in your letter of the 11th inst. is equally unexpected and surprising.

Not knowing the particular charges that are alleged against you, it is impossible for me to make a specific reply, I can therefore only say in general terms that the employments you sustained in the year 1776, and in that period of the year when we experienced our greatest distresses are a proof that you was not suspected by me of infidelity, or want of integrity; for had the least suspicion of the kind reached my mind, either from observation or report, I should most assuredly have marked you out as a fit object of resentment.

While on our retreat through Jersey, I remember your being sent from Newark, to the Assembly of New Jersey, then sitting, to rouse and animate them to spirited measures for our support; and at the same time General Mifflin was sent to Pennsylvania for the same purpose. This employment was certainly a mark of my confidence in you at that time.

Your conduct, so far as it came to my immediate notice, during the short period we lay on the west bank of the Delaware, appeared solicitous for the public good. And your conduct at Princeton evidenced a spirit and zeal, which to me appeared laudable and becoming a man well affected to the cause we were engaged in.

It is rather a disagreeable circumstance, to have private and confidential letters, hastily written as all mine of that class are, upon a supposition that they would remain between the parties only, produced as evidence in a matter of public discussion, but conscious that my public and private sentiments, are at all times alike, I shall not withhold these letters should you think them absolutely necessary to your justification.

If I have in my possession any such letter as you particularly allude to, it is not at present with me—being in the field perfectly light, I have divested myself of all papers, public and private; but such of late date as I thought I might have occasion, in my present situation, to refer to; the others remain at a considerable distance from me.

I am, Dear Sir,

Your obedient and most humble servant,

G. WASHINGTON.

The Hon. Joseph Reed, Esq.

My work is now done. It has gone far beyond the limits, which, when I began to write, I thought would circumscribe it; but it has grown on my hands, and hoping to make an end of these inveterate slanders, I have thought it best to deal with them in detail, and to collate every item of historical evidence, however minute, that I know to exist. I do not hope to have it said that these questions have been discussed in a judicial spirit, for I am conscious of strong feelings which may have affected my judgment. But I am sure that nothing has been intentionally overstated or misrepresented, and no evidence held back which was apparently adverse. If I have been betrayed into asperity of language, let it be borne in mind how dark are the accusations made against my ancestor, that crimes are imputed to him of the deepest hue of guilt, described in the strongest language, and what stealthy and systematic industry has been shown by the living purveyors of calumny, one and all, having for their aim to injure me and mine. If, in anything I have been compelled to say, pain has been given to the living, I mean the innocent living, while it is a matter of great regret, let it be remembered, the re-awakening of these controversies is no work of mine. For more than twenty years have I submitted in silence to periodical revivals of this poisonous rubbish of the past, and I now reluctantly present to the public this vindication of the dead, in justice to my family, and to the Truth of History.

POSTSCRIPT.

I have not thought it worth while to notice Mr. Bancroft's minute criticisms on my 'Biography of Reed.' Looking over the twenty years which have rolled by since the Book was published, I am glad that ill nature can detect so few mistakes. I am tempted however to reproduce the opinions of five eminent American public men, of widely different characters and positions, which at the time gave me—then a young author—great pleasure.

"For a grandson," wrote Albert Gallatin, "you are very reserved and temperate in your estimation of your ancestor's great name. I can assure you, when I entered public life in 1790, his memory was most enthusiastically revered by the party to which I was attached, and I heard various true anecdotes and several suggestions highly honourable to him. Amongst the last was the general belief that the decisive march from Trenton to Princeton was suggested by him. But the great value of your Biography consists in the number of authentic facts and documents, now for the first time published, and which throw much light on the general history of the Revolution."

From Chancellor Kent.

Summit, Essex Co., N. J.. July 9, 1847.

Dear Sir,

I hope you will not take amiss this intrusive note from a stranger. My domicil is the City of New York, but I am here in a country cottage with my family for the summer, and I have just finished the earnest and interesting perusal of your "Life and Correspondence of Joseph Reed," your paternal grandfather, and I feel gratified for the pleasure and instruction you have afforded me by your two volumes. It is a most interesting and admirable history of one of the ablest and purest of patriots of the Revolution. The portraits of President Reed, of Washington, of Greene, are admirable, and they were three of the great actors in the great scenes of that day. I want language to express my sense of their illustrious merits. Your volumes are written with the greatest dignity and truth. I purchased them as soon as they were out and though I took with me Prescott's Peru, I have passed it by as infinitely less interesting than your Memoir. I am a great admirer of contemporary history of these past events with the perfect authenticity that original correspondence affords. I am old enough to recollect vividly the historical events from the battle of Lexington to the present day, and listened when young to all the news, and rumours, and handbills, and newspapers that were shown and read through the early campaigns of the American War, and I have the recollection and feelings of a contemporary. I was driven from New Haven College on the 5th of July, 1779, and fled to my father's house at Fairfield. The next morning, I saw it in flames caused by British incendiaries. I fled to the vicinity of Norwalk where my maternal grandfather's house was burned, and even the humble school house in which I was taught my earliest teachings. In 1781, I left College and was placed in the office of Mr. Benson, the Attorney General of the State, and there I saw from time to time, and listened to the great men who visited there—such as George Clinton, Washington, Hamilton, Lawrence, Schuyler,

Dana, Duane, &c., and imbibed the utmost veneration for such characters. It is no wonder I take such a deep interest in such works as yours—and so I did in 'Gibbs' History of Federalism, during the life of his grandfather, Oliver Wolcott, and in Judge Burnet's History of the N. W. Territory. I consider yours and such histories as monuments of the great men of the Revolutionary Age.

Please excuse this perhaps impertinent narrative, and accept my gratitude for the honour you have done your country, and the pleasure you have afforded by the discharge of filial duty to one of the best and most faultless men that took part in the Revolution.

Believe me to be, with
the highest respect, Y'rs,
JAMES KENT.

From John Sergeant of Pennsylvania.

"I have finished the first volume of the 'Life and Correspondence,' and will be glad to have the second as soon as may be. I have found it very interesting, and the interest to increase as I have gone on. It appears to me that the work will be likely to take a strong hold, and I hope will repay you for your labour. It is a curious history of the details, in their natural proportions, of an eventful period, and of the actual workings of men in times of difficulty and danger, without exaggeration or colouring. The chief figure cannot be said to be brought out. It brings out itself without any effort in the narrative for effect. I am myself surprised at its stature and power as exhibited in a simple, unaffected statement of facts, all authenticated by unquestioned evidence."

Mr. Calhoun, wrote to me from Fort Hill, in South Carolina, on the 6th of November, 1847:

"I have devoted my first leisure hours to the perusal of your work, and have just finished it. I am greatly indebted for the information and pleasure it afforded. It gives fuller and more accurate information of some of the most important occurrences of the Revolution, and of the character of many of the principal actors in that great drama. High as my opinion was of your distinguished ancestor, the perusal of this work has raised him still higher in my estimation. His letters are his best eulogist, and will ever place him in the first rank of the great men who achieved our Independence, for talent, integrity, devoted patriotism, and important services rendered to the cause and country."

Lastly, from Mr. Sparks, to whose kind offices I was deeply indebted, and whose gentle and tolerant judgment on all vexed historical questions is so strongly in contrast with the carping asperities of these times, I received this characteristic note:

Cambridge, September 24, 1847.

"I obtained a copy of your work as soon as it came out, and looked it through, and read parts of it carefully. The opinion which I had formed of the first volume was sustained to the end. It is a valuable collection of new historical materials, and put together with singular good judgment, conveying clear and accurate impressions of characters and facts. I know of no work of this class of more successful execution. In my opinion, it is a model of historical biography. The moderation and candour with which you have touched upon controverted points, or rather the heats of local and temporary politics, must defeat all the aims of ill natured criticism, if any are disposed to criticise in this temper."

And he adds, speaking of the Cadwalader affair:

"I think you are quite wise in letting all those old matters sleep. Your book will stand on its merits. It needs no props."

I hesitate to add the following which gratified me once, but which has no value now:

"I must renew to you my thanks for your most valuable volumes. They form the most important contribution to American Revolutionary History which has been made for many years. In performing a duty towards the memory of your ancestor, you have not failed to do a good service to your country. Let me say again how much I am obliged to you for your volumes, partly as a token of your regard, still more as an American and a student of our history, happy in everything that illustrates it so elaborately and so well."

Very truly,
Your obliged,
GEORGE BANCROFT.

London, February 1st, 1848.

THE END.

Printed in Poland
by Amazon Fulfillment
Poland Sp. z o.o., Wrocław

68552981R00074